The Roan

A Fictionalized Story Giving Voice
to the Past by Retelling a
Grandmother's History

Shirely F. B. Carter

Goose River Press
Waldoboro, Maine

Library of Congress Card Number: 2012941002

ISBN 13: 978-1-59713-124-7

First Printing, 2012

Published by
Goose River Press
3400 Friendship Road
Waldoboro ME 04572
e-mail: gooseriverpress@roadrunner.com
www.gooseriverpress.com

To My Family

Those before me, those born at the time I was born, those to whom I gave birth, their children and those to come.

Contents

Acknowledgments

I owe my greatest respect and appreciation to my maternal grandmother, Laura Frances Washington Rickards, who told the stories and began the traditions. She cooked everything from scratch. Thanksgiving turkey took most of the morning into early afternoon. My sister Audrey when she was very young went to Gram's house and sped up the long process. Audrey and I have maintained those cooking traditions and have passed them along to all of our children: both male and female. Gram's respect for education and her fortitude has also been passed on through the family.

I thank my daughters, Laura and Mia, along with their cousins who have inspired and supported me through these many years of research. Laura and I have traveled to Virginia to the Lee Mansion, written to historical repositories to collect data, and driven to Groton to locate Mary Jane Lee Washington's brush covered grave.

Much thanks and appreciation goes to my researcher cousins, Norma Munroe and Peter Chester. They drove from Connecticut to my home in Massachusetts, bringing a hearty home cooked meal to sustain us while we spent the day exchanging and identifying photos, comparing oral history, legends and documents.

Deep gratitude is owed my younger cousin, Lorraine Sanders of California, who arranged a spectacular gathering of researcher "cousins" right at the Washington homestead in Hyannis Port, MA. The house and property were still owned and occupied by the children and grandchildren of George and Mary Jane Lee Washington. It was at this wonderful gathering that I discovered where my great grandmother was buried. My grandmother evaded my direct inquiries about her mother's death and burial place with vague answers such as, "some things are difficult to explain."

When my grandmother's youngest daughter Evelyn was still alive, she showed great patience answering my many questions about how I was related to the many folks in Leominster, Boston, and Somerville. We called her Aunt Evvie and she corresponded with many of the relatives, knew intimate family stories like the names of family pets, and who was known to be clairvoyant.

I am aware that I may not be able to credit all those who deserve to be acknowledged, so I will apologize in advance and list those folks in the Worcester Public Library and the Sturgis Library on Cape Cod for their help and direction. Other folks like the town clerks and Isabelle Beale keeper of records at the Groton Private Cemetery, Mary Ellen Cooper in the records office at Tewksbury Hospital, all deserve to be acknowledged for their generous contributions of time and attention. I was seeking records from the eighteen hundreds and they found them.

I owe a debt of thanks to editorial advisors: Jan Sadler, Jayanti Tamm and Catherine Sarytchoff.

I thank my relatives and friends who read the drafts and a special thanks to Kira Beaudoin who designed the covers of both my published works. There are thanks due also to horse ranchers: Victoria Givins, Kimberly Moore, Dorothy Roberts, Tamela Denault and Dale Anderson who gave consent to use images of horses from their web pages to use on this book's cover.

The Roan

Chapter One

The Roan

The spirits gave Mary Jane her vision before the fatal blow that crushed her nose, gashed her forehead and left her slowly drifting away from this strange, cold place. She saw the vision in the shadows made by the bare tree branches that danced on the path. She heard it in the labored, frosty breath of the horses that pulled the pungs, matting the snow, making it easier to walk out of doors. Mary Jane knew she would never see the Hollow again. The blood that once seeped from her wound continued inside her skull: slowly stealing her earthly presence, forcing old sounds, old memories to surface and fade like shimmering waves on moonlit water.

How could she tell anyone how slaves see things and know things? They weren't even able to see the ordinary. Mary Jane didn't correct the admissions clerk when he made his notations on June 15, 1896.[1]

"What do we have here? Hmm, a white female...fairly developed but a bit emaciated, feeble, about fifty-five years old. You say she's taken to running away?"

Mary Jane said not a word. Her thoughts drifted. She recalled the sound of hounds and thought about her

---

[1]Medical Records Tewksbury Hospital for Mary Jane Lee Washington, The Commonwealth of Massachusetts Executive Office of Human Services Department of Public Health 150 Tremont Street, Boston 02111. Mary Ellen Cooper obtained via Michael Price, Deputy General Counsel.

grandmother peering in the window, thinking she would be calming her, telling her not to fret. They would soon be free and safe forever.

***

Mary Jane's youngest daughter, my maternal grandmother Laura Washington Rickards, walked quickly to the institution lobby. Her corseted torso caused her to appear taller than her sixty-five inches. She wore her best grey wool winter coat. It fell to the top of her black boots. Under her coat, she wore her Sunday best blue paisley print dress. Bright red poppies circled her broad rimmed black felt hat. A thin grey wool scarf covered her hat, securing it from the wind and covering her braided hair and supple neck. Laura's face was rigid with pain and ruddy from the bitter December wind. She slid the scarf onto her shoulders and searched the lobby for a familiar face.

She spoke to her brothers, "Dead! Mother is dead? Murdered in this vile place? Two weeks, just two weeks and she's gone! Dan, I can never forgive you. You said you'd take care of her! Why? For the love of heaven why?" Her choking sobs were muted, deep in her throat.

Dan attempted to explain, "Pa couldn't look after her and work the farm too. She got so confused, and headstrong. No way could we keep up with her running off and putting the wash into the tubs of maple sap." As he stepped forward to comfort her, his sister flailed her thick black gloves across his chest. "Laura, I don't know how you managed. I didn't know what else to do-with you losing both your girls. I just couldn't put more on you. This is too terrible. Who could have known? Dear

Laura I'm so sorry." His sad, dry eyes were sunken and bore dark shadows like half moons onto his cheeks. Clear mucus ran in a stream from his nose. The rumpled handkerchief he used to control the flow shielded his face from her tear-filled gaze. The grief pained him such that he became immobile, a gaunt statue with proud, sculptured cheekbones and lean muscular body. Three siblings stood in silence, their collective sadness as bitter and cold as the December evening.

Laura Rickards, Dan and George Washington arrived at Tewsksbury on December 30, 1896. The ride from Malden consumed most of Laura's day. Brother George had come up from the Hollow in Hyannis, stayed overnight with Dan in Watertown. Their father George Washington, the elder, remained on Cape Cod to tend the farm. The brothers were already at the Almshouse when Laura arrived. The nursing supervisor attempted to offer comforting words.

"She didn't appear to suffer. We are so sorry for your loss. You say the mortician in Groton will care for her remains? Is there anything more I can do for you?"

Laura spoke gravely. "Tell me what happened, every detail!"

"Well, there isn't much to tell." The nurse spoke slowly, pausing as she watched their agonized faces. "Our nurses treated her bruise immediately after she was stuck. We sent notice to the family, but this demise was never anticipated. We called in a specialist to make certain her face would not be marred. She's been in the infirmary and was given the best of care. Her wounds healed quickly and well." The supervisor said no more to the family. She summoned an attendant who was instructed to escort them to the Infirmary where Mary

Jane's body still remained.

The Nursing Supervisor had given the family a much abbreviated version of the actual events.

***

"What happened here?" The supervisor was more annoyed than upset.

She had hurried from her office off the day hall where patients were seated after being aroused from the sleeping area. The day hall was a smaller open area, only separated from the sleeping area by long rows of low partitions. While standing, one could survey the entire unit from the day hall.

"Mrs. Washington was just sitting there. She's so weak she can't stand at the window much. We sash her in the chair for fear she'll tumble. Then Mandy Nations just hauled off and struck Mrs. Washington in the face! It happened so fast, no warning..."

"This is your ward, and you are responsible for whatever goes on here. The gauze bandage has stopped the bleeding. Clean all the blood off her face. It's not likely to be nearly as bad as it seems. Face wounds are always bloody. We don't want her to scar. You know this requires an incident report. Did you put Mandy in seclusion? Get that paper work finished before you go home! I'm calling our specialist, Dr. Irish. He'll fix her up just fine. Get a hold of yourself, Miss Leary!"

The attendant's hands trembled as she sponged the damp blood that trailed from Mary Jane's forehead, down her sharp cheekbone, and under her chin, where a large stain gathered on the gray shawl covering her frail shoulders. Mary Jane's gaze was fixed, her once strong body, motionless. That night she slept in the infirmary on the upper levels of the hospital.[2]

Mary Jane studiously collected herself and in silence recalled how the morning sun shrouded by snow clouds cast gray shadows over the countryside. This isolated parcel of land in Tewksbury, Massachusetts was selected purposefully, far away from the town. The architectural plans for Almshouses and Insane Asylums look much the same: clusters of stately brick buildings, out in the countryside, with ample land for gardening, herding, with independent water and fuel supplies. Mary Jane Lee Washington had been remanded to the benevolent care of the State in June of 1896. This decision had been reluctantly made by one of her sons, Daniel. He confided in the men, but hid his feelings of helplessness and frustration from his sisters: Carrie, Sarah, Zilpha, Helen and Laura. Neither my grandmother Laura nor my great aunts ever spoke of the sad circumstance. I found the details in the hospital records.

***

It was nearly noontime, on the second of December when Dr. Irish examined the wounds. He snipped the bulky, bloodstained bandage and spoke to Mary Jane.

"Miss Washington, you've got quite a black eye! I want to check your wound. I don't expect it will hurt very much." He turned to the aide and inquired, "Is she taking nourishment? She seems so frail and weak." the doctor did not give the aide opportunity to respond. He stared at Mary Jane and asked in a loud voice, "How are

---

[2]Ibid.

5

you feeling today Miss?" There was something about the way she stared at him: a knowing, sage look of defiance. She held his eye and said nothing. He turned again to the aide. "How long has she been like this?" He no longer directed questions at his stoic patient. Mary Jane stared at him, following his every move with rapt attention.

"She's been here since June," the aid apologetically explained, "She used to be up and about—" Dr. Irish interrupted the aide.

"Get me a cut down and some dextrose and water. She needs to be hydrated."

The aid turned to get the fluids, but the doctor summoned her. "Stay right here until I look at this gash. I think her nose is broken. The cranial bone is in tact. My, it's a large wound. Get me Iodine, lots of gauze and a suture set, oh, and some liquid cocaine. I'll try to numb this a bit before I sew her up. Miss? Miss, does this hurt?"

Mary Jane gave him a bold stare. It worried him.

"Doesn't she ever speak?"

"Well no, not since she was struck," the aid answered hesitantly. "She used to wander away and run off, saying she was going to the hollow. We couldn't let her out on the grounds. Then she would stand looking out the windows for long periods." The aide rapidly gathered the fluids and sterile suture set from the wooden cupboard in the room. "We had to sash her in her chair when she got weak. Otherwise, she was never a real problem...a genteel lady, soft spoken. She only seems to brighten up and converse when her sons come to visit. They haven't been here in a spell. She gets restless when they leave, and tries to run off again."

Dr. Irish barely listened to the information he

6

requested. He explored and cleaned the large skin flap, muttering to himself. "Periostium is clean, right front parietal intact, right eyelid needs fine silk suture. Her arms and fingers are twitching. Pain, perhaps, hmm, that should do it. She won't even have a scar."

The patient remained attentive yet silent, as the dextrose flowed directly into her vein. She was still in the infirmary when he returned more than a week later.

"How are you feeling Mrs. Washington? I've come to remove those sutures." The male attendant answered for Mary Jane.

"Oh she seems all right. She certainly doesn't complain. It's like she just checks on us, testing to see if we are doing a good job." He smiled affectionately at his compliant patient, knowing she studied his every move. "We can't keep her up in a chair for long. She dozes off. We have to wake her to take her medicine and she has no appetite." Dr. Irish had already removed the bandage and was pleased to see a clean wound. As he had anticipated, once he removed the stitches, there was barely a trace of a scar. Internally, the catastrophe never ended. The damage remained unseen. Subdural hematomas still confounded medical practitioners at that time. Mary Jane Washington's death certificate states her cause of death was "debility."[3]

***

[3]Death Certificate for Mary Jane Lee Washington, December 30, 1896, The Commonwealth of Massachusetts, Town of Tewksbury. Copy in possession of author.

December had near passed when the house physician was summoned again to the Infirmary. He arrived promptly and greeted the aide who explained the urgency.

"Doctor, she's become much debilitated since the head injury. She's not been herself. Nair speaks a word. She took no sustenance today, simply stopped breathing."

After searching for a pulse and placing his stethoscope on her chest, the doctor declared, "Well she's expired... no rigor yet. Has the family been notified?"

"We sent word she was failing. The relatives planned to visit again after the holidays. It will be difficult if they arrive today. One of the daughters came last visit and nearly fainted away. It seems the sons had not told the rest of the family that their mother was in our care."

The doctor had no patience to listen to the details. He barked his final orders and set about his paperwork. "You'd best get all your charts in order. You will need more than the usual mortuary forms. This incident will become a legal matter."

On that fateful December evening, George, Dan, and Laura proceeded to the infirmary, behind the attendant. They gazed at their mother and spoke farewells with their eyes. Laura moved to the bedside. Mary Jane Washington's countenance was that of a sleeping child. In disbelief, Laura held her mother's familiar hand, expecting to feel warmth. Instead she felt coldness, stiff fingers curled inward like the claw of a dead bird.

In the winter of 1896, Tewksbury, Massachusetts there was no warmth.

***

It was nearly two weeks before the weather became mild enough for the Groton Cemetery to bury their mother. Solace and silence were the order of the day. Each sibling colluded in this mode of grief.

Laura surely wondered how this could have happened. Did the woman who attacked her mother know what she was doing? Why weren't the attendants aware that this person was dangerous? They knew how gentle her Mother was. Surely, her mother never provoked anyone. Perhaps no one will ever know. Laura's mother overcame so many trials and challenges. She so loved the warmth and closeness of her family in Maryland. If only the war didn't change things, they all might be there now. A slave's life was never easy, yet my great grandmother was said to have spoken fondly of the south, the land, and the times. The family returned after the war. It's so strange that Mary Jane Lee's life should end in a cold place like Tewksbury, a place so far from where her life began.

Laura's husband Elias encouraged her to move closer to him and Daniel, who stood alone behind the women and their husbands. Laura stood rigid, lost in thought. Elias reached over to her, but Laura had detached herself from her surroundings. Elias was a dapper, brown skin man, shorter than the Washington brothers: a well-proportioned man with stately carriage. His black derby hat, with its narrow brim, exposed his full features, trim moustache and well-groomed short beard. His dark gray coat was trimmed with a beaver collar. Elias held his gaze on his wife, while other couples huddled together: their adult children surrounding them.

Daniel's worn black coat hung loosely on his tall, lean, muscular body. His broad brimmed black felt hat, warped with wear, rested jauntily on his bowed head: shielding his face from view. Elias thought about poor Dan. He was the only unmarried one and he seemed so distraught. It was as if Dan had taken on this whole tragedy, as if it was of his making. The whole family noticed the changes in Mother Washington. None of them could have predicted this outcome.

These are secrets families keep out of grief and embarrassment. Dan in particular appeared to hold onto the grief until his life's end. My memory of him is that of a somber, silent person with a leg amputation. He visited Ellen Street but spent the end of his life in a room at Aunt Helen's on Tremont Street in Boston. He never spoke and we children were ushered by the cloth covered doorway of his room.

When the brief Bible reading was over, the group dispersed as planned, to gather at sister Zilpha's house in Pepperell. Her home, with its large welcoming porch, was nearest the Groton cemetery. Neighbors and friends prepared a hot meal for the family. Susan Shattuck, Laura's close childhood friend offered condolences.

"I know Laura, as the youngest child, you have been close to your mother even since your marriage. I'm so sorry Laura, so very sorry."

Laura could barely look at her friend as she nodded in agreement. Families quickly assembled to journey home to Boston, Leominster, and down to Cape Cod. Elias draped the carriage blanket snug over their legs then wrapped his arm around her shoulders. In silence the whole way home, Laura agonized about her mother's life. She stared out of the carriage window, barely noticing the few lighted houses and thick groves of trees.

She recalled how her mother found dignity in her

work as a slave. She had good feelings about the south, even about the people who owned her. Mary Jane Lee was always proud of her father, as unfathomable as their lives were. She had to struggle to adjust to freedom in the north and never shied away from hard work. Laura thought it was unfair! However did her mother manage to stay so content and pleased with all her children? Could she ever be as devoted a wife and mother? Laura's mother believed a woman's role in life was to bear and forebear: something once heard in a dream. She accepted all hardships with such grace and hope. Now her mother lies in this cold place forever. Laura felt a heavy loss. She would no longer have her Mother's counsel, never again be consoled by her, never hear her tell of her life on the plantation, the stories about people and places she loved. Laura vowed to bear witness to her mother's life and never forget what her mother had given her, never forget what she told her, never forget, never!

Chapter Two

Filly

The land sloping below the bluff was hot, steamy, moist, embracing all living things in sparkling mist. Perspiration beaded on muscles at rest, and brows during sleep. In order to make something, or to do something, required special concentration and dedication: a single mindedness that signified a quest.

There were many summer nights like this, yet this evening in August of 1828, a sense of urgency floated with the fragrance of the white blossoms adorning the scattered trees. Both on the high plains of the Lee plantation and down on the water's edge, the basin-like back land of the Fleming plantation, the air hung, pungent, evoking a queasiness of the entrails with its sweetness. All of nature was calm and still. Man and beast were lolling, fanning, retreating to the shaded corners of the earth. Plantations seemed abandoned.

A curious, muted clopping came from the water's edge, softly sucking then thumping rhythmically up the grassy plain that separated the Fleming manor house from the slave quarters. A row of miniature lean-to's, amazing imitations of habitations, snuggled next to the large stone larder shed and the summer kitchen with its great open-air hearth. The filly trotted to the last shanty. The gaping windows draped with gauzy folds of cloth unmoved in the still air, shimmered a pale pink; a stealthy beauty bestowed by the redness of the setting

sun, already sinking into the sullen grayness of night.
The horse snorted, puncturing the air with sound and specks of spittle that fell unnoticed. Her sleek withers were shining, streaked with streamlets running down to her muddied hooves. Froth clung to her gaping mouth, moving with each stolid breath. The rider dismounted, first peering, and then latching his gaze on the silhouette of the girl. Skokien stood there in the half-light, her slim body defining the perfection of femininity that an artist might cleverly design from mahogany. Perspiration on her rich cocoa skin radiated, exposing all of nature's exquisite design. Her cloth wrap thinly veiled her budding breasts and exposed her firm jutting shoulders. Its brown tones matched the reddish soil. The wrap flowed freely from a simple fold tucked at her armpit. The rider's loins seized, events followed: not invisible, but unseen and unacknowledged.

Birthin' Day

The month of May came quickly for Skokien. The warm Maryland sun rose earlier each day, stretching the morning and allowing the servants to cook the evening meal outside in the summer kitchen. Not much else was new on the Fleming Plantation. The aroma of baking bread served as first call to dinner. Following routine, the old man rang the bell, while the others finished their familiar chores. It was Skokien who dragged the bread from the hot coals, skillfully slanting the paddle and sliding the hot tin onto a large stone table. The earthen floor nearly circled the massive fireplace, and the girl carefully rested her paddle off the soil onto the stone hearth. She peered down at her bare toes, extending her slim leg to improve her view. Her foot was large. Skokien folded her arms across the small mound that protruded immediately under her bosom. Her gaze drifted about this familiar kitchen as if seeing it for the first time.

Stout joists abutted the partially flag-stoned floor and stretched upward to suspend the sloping roof. The kitchen had no solid walls. Cast iron tongs, pokers, pots and kettles adorned the timbers nearest the fireplace. Its mammoth chimney rose above the roof, sending both smoke and heat into the evening air.

Someone came and took the bread over to the manor house. Skokien fixed her gaze on the coals.

"I wonder if my body will stay big. She mused. A sudden flutter in her belly, followed by a fierce cramping, seized her full attention.

"Oh my. Is this it?" Her eyes roved around now, looking for Ma Molly, her helpmate and confidant. Throughout the winter months, she and Ma Molly worked side by side in the kitchen at the big house. Skokien, confident in cooking, relied less and less on Ma Molly for direction. It was birthing that she wanted instruction on now. Only a few of the servants were aware of Skokien's condition. Ma Molly being the first, had already answered a raft of Skokien's questions, and right away guessed why they were being asked. Another sharp cramp in her belly came accompanied by knife-like jabs gripping both flanks. She spoke aloud.

"Oh—oh Ma Molly!" No answer came. The silence startled the girl into frightening awareness. "Oh Lawdy, they all ova' servin' dinna. Bread gone!" Jolting into motion, Skokien left the kitchen, sprinted past the larder shed and turned onto the dirt path leading to the shanty. Tiny beads of perspiration caused her face to shine. Her crowned hair and wide unblinking eyes gave her face

14

a mask-like beauty found only on mummies of Nubian queens. She stopped abruptly on the threshold. The pain peaked, forcing a surprising flood of warm fluid to gush down her legs and darken the soil.

"Ohhh, Lawdy—ma waters—muss be ma waters. Smell like sweet grass. Chile, this be yo' birthin' day." She spoke aloud although no person could hear her. As the next sharp stabs tore from her flanks to her loins and back to her belly, Skokien's thoughts took flight.

She did not remember crawling to her cot and never saw the sanguine stains now seeping onto it. She heard a female voice from her past speaking firmly, telling her she would come of an age when she would bear and forbear. A softer male voice assured her, that the baby would be theirs, they would share it. The voice continued, assuring her of his care and concern, promising to return as often possible. Her soul filled with doubt. In her reverie, she found herself pleading, asking for assurance, doubting he would ever return. Her heart pounded like a racing horse, she could see it, a reddish horse, flecked with white, making the color shimmer. The sound of its heavy breathing filled the room. Then with one unearthly whinny, it vanished.

"Wha's wrong with you girl?" Ma Molly stroked the girl's brow as she spoke.

"Firs ah done think yo dead, o' juss gone off somewhere in yo' mine. Come back to us Skokie, please come back!"

Lil' Momma

"Yo show give me a fright, Skokie." Ma Molly patted the girl's brow with a damp cloth. A single candle illuminated the sparsely furnished shanty. The tall yellow flame waved in the evening breeze. The older woman sat quietly on a low stool near the girl's mat and rested her elbow on a nearby crate draped with a pale yellow cloth.

"Ma Molly," Skokien whispered, "the baby come? Is it..."

"Done fret now. The baby girl juss fine." Interrupted Molly. "She small and palish, an done more hollerin than the Missus baby done all winta. Now, you sip some 'o 'dis broth. Get some strength into yo'self." Molly's large, bony features etched a shadow over the girl's mat as she offered the bowl to Skokien.

"No, no." Skokien protested loudly. Where's ma baby at? Bring her to me. You say she' a girl?" Now propped on her elbow, Skokien turned, moving off her bed mat.

"Oh my, oooh my! This room's turning like a whirl pool." The young woman dropped backwards, rumpling the thin cloth that covered her torso.

"Water still comin' outa me. An you already freshened my bed, an the cover too? 'Dis bed be ruined!"

Molly sprang to her feet. With a worried moan, she placed her massive hands on Skokien's abdomen. She feared the girl's uterus had gone soft and she would bleed out.

"Stop! Please stop." Skokien pleaded, "Yo' pouncin' on me like a tub 'o bread dough!"

Grim faced and ignoring the girl's pleas, the old woman continued to roll and push Skokien's belly as if she were kneading bread!

"Put yo' hans here, chile. If'n yo' done' feel dis hard ball, we both gwan be pouncin' yo' belly."

Still arguing, but no longer able to resist her helper's vigilant attention, Skokien sipped the broth and drifted into a peaceful somnolence. The muted whimpers of her infant brought a smile to her face. The swaddled baby was tucked in a large reed basket by the door. The breeze carried the baby's cries into the night. Ma Molly did not take her eyes from the girl, even when she heard a bustle of skirts in the doorway.

A small, brown-skin woman with a ready smile hovered around like a little butterfly. "How she doin' Molly?" Tillylish asked.

"She be restin' now, she need her ress. Shore wish she'd taken more broth. Long as her belly stay hard, she be alright." Ma Molly spoke pensively, as if she were alone with the girl. Tillylish quietly tended the baby as Dahl, a sad-faced woman, brought another stool and sat down by the door.

"Molly," Tillylish complained, "Dis baby ain't takin' to spoon water. Be right good if'n Skokie's milk come in quick." Dahl almost smiled, when she peeked at the newborn infant Tillylish gently placed on her lap.

"Whass happen to Skokie?" Dahl asked. Ma Molly only sighed. Un-offended, Dahl kept talking. "We all finish at the Manna house. Miss Flemin, she ask 'bout Skokie. She spectin' Skokie to be her nursemaid for 'lil Missy Jane when she start totterin' around this fall."

"What yo tell Miss Flemin?" snapped Ma Molly. Her piercing inquiry met with a strained silence. Dahl rose, moving into the doorway.

"Set down, Dahl. I juss been worryin' 'bout Sokie." Ma Molly admonished.

"I ain't said nothin' warn't true!" Dahl exclaimed.

"You ain't said nothin' wrong—no matter what yo' tole' Miss Flemin." Ma Molly looked wearily at the small cluster of women.

Sophie had joined them. "I heared the chile and fig-

17

ure everythin' all right down here. What yoall' fussin' 'bout? Dahl, yo' all right?"

Dahl looked at Ma Molly.

"Oh, we alright..." Ma Molly assured. Her intensity had silenced Dahl and Tillylish. Ma Molly explained.

"Miss Flemin askin' bout Skokie...wantin' her waiting on Missy Jane, an cookin' too, I 'spect. When cool weather come, Skokien be ready. We all put in some time helpin' Skokie with this little one, juss' like the ole one's did when Skokie's momma got sole." Ma Molly continued to stare across the room at Skokien, dismissing the others, she drifted into her own thoughts and remembrances. The slave women knew how Skokien's momma would run, taking chances, coming back and forth to see that her child was coming up good. No one had seen Falashaday for nigh on two winters. Ma Molly offered a silent prayer, that she was somewhere safe up north.

The infant squirmed and yowled as Dahl pressed her close. Now that the silence was ruptured by staccato howls, Sophie took charge of the somber group. "Skokie momma likely dead by now. Dat gal, Falashaday, ain't never stop runnin'. 'Dose swamp injuns give her mo dan time away from Buchanan fields, precious chile—'fore Skokie ever know her momma, she gone. Fiel' hands all hard peoples, but dat women warn't scared o' nuthin, not even death! An Skokie's daddy never seen no plantation."

"An ain't nobody but Falashaday ever seen him."

"Lawdy," quipped Sophie, "dis baby fixin to wake the dead with her yowlin'." Sophie, a buxom woman with black eyes and charcoal skin, took the baby, snuggled it to her bosom and began to sing. "Climb—in 'up d' mountain—children. Did-n't come here to stay. If ah nev-er-more see you a-gain,—gon-na meet you at d'jud-ment day—Hmmm, hmmm."[1] Sophie kept humming even as the baby quieted.

"Molly," Sophie commanded, "You drink-a-'dat broth an stretch out ova here. We goin' to set dis place straight an den we all ress. Dat 'ole sun be up 'fore the breeze cool dis place."

Without protest, Molly sipped the broth, staring blankly at the sleeping young woman on the mat. "She ashy but restin' good." Checking once more, Molly leaned over her young charge. "Belly hard." Assuring only herself, Ma Molly stretched out on the mat Dahl had prepared. Sleep overcame her before Dahl and Tillylish said their good nights.

Skokien roused to Sophie's continued humming. "Sophie? Sophie, please bring ma baby girl here."

"It sure do my heart good to hear yo' soun', Skokien," beamed Sophie. "Put dis chile right onto yo' breast. Don't be worryin' 'bout milk. This young one get water out 'a stone: she so feisty." Sophie chuckled as she lay the baby on Skokie's chest. "Dahl 'n me goin' to fix dis place come sun up. When we all go to chores, you just move over Ma Molly place. We done took all of the birthin' cloths for they ripen in 'd heat." Sophie's ebony face beamed broadly, like the morning sun splendering the hilltops.

"Mornin li'l momma," Sophie crooned, as she left the cabin and melted into the night.

---

[1]Boyer, H.C. "Climbin' Up D' Mountain," Lift Every Voice and Sing 11. New York, NY.: The Church Pension Fund, 1993

19

Namin' Day

Only a week and a day passed before Skokien was seen at the big house cheerfully taking charge of all of her duties. She set the table for breakfast, put the already leavened bread into the brick oven, and then went to the bedchambers to empty the slops and the basins used for morning freshening up. Next, she straightened the linen, fluffing the feather-filled pillows, and drew the heavy tapestry drapes wide open to let in the morning light.

Mrs. Fleming had missed Skokien's usual scurrying. Little Miss Janie had asked for her too. The little one had come into the kitchen to bid for more jam and hot bread. Her mother followed in order to steady the toddler's unsteady gait and to instruct the servants.

Mrs. Fleming heard Skokien's quick footsteps as the girl scurried up and down the pantry stairs. These stairs were off the kitchen and led to the hallway outside the master bedroom and the nursery. Ma Molly always mounted the stairs with a slow, sturdy shuffle, careful to hold her skirts and petticoats from causing her to trip. Not Skokien, she nearly always raced, with one hand full of linens or a bucket, her skirts lumped in a wad under her armpit. "Well, Missy Skokie," Mrs. Fleming mimicked little Janie's usual greeting to Skokien, "What kept you from your chores these last few days?"

Skokien smiled and admitted, "I was feelin' poorly for a day or so. I'm fine now."

Mrs. Fleming already knew the reason. She'd heard the female slaves joyfully gossiping in the kitchen, and admired how loyal and nurturing the older women were towards Skokien, much like they were when Skokien herself was a newborn. The elusive runaway, who brought Skokien into the world, trusted the Fleming household—both slaves and owners. She knew her baby would be cared for and might never be sold off. The Flemings weren't like many of the other frightened plantation owners. The Fleming chattel was assigned to managing the manor house, the grounds, the stables and the large garden that fed them all. Their tobacco fields were no longer maintained for income. Mr. Fleming, a civil servant, worked at the Court House in Baltimore. Harold would over night at his father's Baltimore home, where they spent most of their visits talking about the strategies and boldness of the men from Great Britain. He never shared war stories with his wife.

While Harold was away, his wife, Jane Wellington Fleming, managed the estate. She relied on her slaves, who provided reliable help, amusement and sometimes, comfort. She inherited the older slaves from her mother. The women had cared for her throughout her youth and old Moses was smithing in his younger days on the Wellington Plantation. Mrs. Fleming had asked Moses if he would like to "hire out" and work his trade, but Moses would have no part of it. There was not a plantation in all of Maryland he was willing to chance...and be sold off. He settled for tending the horses, cows, chickens and pigs and managing the farm, with a little help from the females.

Harold's family did not own slaves and he knew little about managing a large tobacco plantation. His education prepared him for the bar and his father sometimes teased him, "You're giving up soldiering to take silk?" British lawyers were considered members of the King's Council, a less dangerous and adventuresome living compared to the military. For all their talk of the British as enemy, both men admired the skill and bravery of the British men they encountered.

Young Harold was respected for his family name and his brief military career. Less than forty-five years before, Harold Fleming Senior fought in the Revolutionary War. Young Harold made his family proud by continuing the tradition with his own service in the military. And now, in the summer of 1829, echoes of war and the need for experienced officers were being discussed.

***

Skokien completed her chores in the bedrooms and nursery. As she descended the stairs she noticed her mistress staring at her.

Mrs. Fleming's broad smile showed respect and humor when she asked Skokien, "And what will you name our sweet Araminta?[2]

"Oh, Miss Flemin, yo know 'bout my birthin day!" Skokien was surprised yet relived to discover her Mistress knew of her delivery. "She' never be call' Araminta. I hope it don'e offen yo, Missus, but I'm fixin' to name her Mary Jane."

When the long day ended, Skokien fetched her baby from the barn, where Moses had been watching over the young one as she slept or howled. The child disturbed no one, and was fed each time Skokie completed an outdoor chore. Skokien hurried to the slave quarters and shouted to Ma Molly, "Ma Molly yo' never believe what Missus Flemin tole me t'day!" Breathless, she tumbled into

---

[2]Araminta, pronounced AERahMintah: Harriet Tubman's birth name, frequently used for slave baby girls.

Molly's cabin, resting the baby's reed basket gently on the floor. "She knew 'bout my little one. She' pleased I'm fixin' to name her Mary Jane, Mary Jane Lee!"

Unable to get a word in, Molly just smiled at the joyful young mother. Ma Molly was resting on her mat. She'd left the Manor house directly after the evening meal, relieved that Skokien would do the cleaning up as had been her duty before the baby came. She watched as Skokien quieted the baby, lifting her and holding her snugly.

"Did I say it all? Missus Flemin' say I can bring Mary Jane to the Big House wid' me every day! Yo' b'leave 'dat Ma Molly?"

Molly chuckled, "Yo' a picture o' joy, Skokie. Seems I'll be missin' peepin' in on ma little one. Them chickens won't be squawkin' when she hungry. They' be missin' her too! Less make dis comin' Sabbath her namin' day! We'gonna' have one fine celebration. Us women can make a feast like we ain't had since Christmas! Baby Mary Jane is goin' to have her a namin' day!"

The women gathered kitchen morsels, garden succulents, old wine, and honey cakes. The slave mother and baby brightened the entire summer. Even Little Missy Janie at the Manor, looked forward to watching baby Mary Jane. She often crooned little tunes, imitating ones she had learned from Sophie. As baby Mary Jane grew, Moses remained care taker of Skokien's young one. The baby loved the out of doors and felt at home in the barn long after she left the cradle. The seasons changed while the routines at the manor house became predictable and quite comfortable.

Chapter Three

Bobby Lee

The family legend regarding Mary Jane Lee's birth never mentioned her slave mother's name. I named her Skokien, a Swahili contraction meaning bubbling home-made brown sugar hooch. It was always stated proudly that her father was General Robert E. Lee. My grand-mother possessed glass slides of his likeness that need authentication. The claim and the legend persist and are recorded in Cape Cod history.[1]

***

Three summers had passed when Ma Molly asked, "He still comin' around, Skokie?"

Ma Molly missed the horse and rider who'd become a familiar sight on holidays and occasional Sundays. The larger than usual harvest and threat of frost had pulled all the servants out to the fields. Skokien was in charge of the Manor house. She and baby Mary Jane slept in the garret except on the Sabbath, her day off.

"He 'takin' to baby Mary Jane. He came 'round juss' this pass' Sunday."

Ma Molly stated the facts as she saw them. "Dat red hair an palish skin less him claim her wid pride."

---

[1]Town of Barnstable. The Seven Villages of Barnstable, (Town of Barnstable, Massachusetts, 1976) 469-470.

Mary Jane Lee was undoubtedly a handsome child. Slave women all over Maryland and Virginia were delivering pale babies. Slave trade restrictions prompted slave owners to "breed" their chattel and to kidnap free blacks, to sell in the deep South.[2] Black mothers had fair-skinned children and white slave owning mothers shared their resources with their husband's bastard children: half sisters and brothers, one slave, the other free...and white.

Araminta

"Well, Skokien, I understand we now have a sweet Araminta in our midst." Harold greeted the baby with a broad smile and handed a small package to Skokien.

"No, Massa Flemin', we has a chile' name Mary Jane: Mary Jane Lee." She spoke with such pride that it made Harold confused. In his attempt to show his pleasure, he heard a touch of contrariness in this young mother's voice. He said no more, and left them. Skokien clutched the package to her breast and beamed at her sleeping child.

It was after the evening meal when the servants retired to the kitchen and Skokien took Mistress Janie off to the nursery, that Harold addressed the incident with his wife. "Dear wife, can you help me understand this situation with Skokie's infant? She boldly told me the child carries our family given names, yet not our surname. Lee? Does this mean the child is Lee chattel? Are we to make payment or inform the widow?"

---

[2]Thomas L. Doughton, "In the Calaboose: Children Kidnapped from Worcester County and Communities of People of Color in Central Massachusetts in 1893" (Short Version, Draft), 1998.

Property rights were a particular point of contention in those days.

"Dear Harold, no need for alarm. Skokien is but a child herself. The Gods smiled on us when she was dropped here—when it could have cost us dearly, harboring the child of a suspected run away!" Their safety and reputation were at issue. Righteous slave owners were threatening anyone appearing unsympathetic to their point of view and would have been impressed if the Flemings were breeding their slaves.

Harold replied, "It seems we have a fair skinned darkie all the same. Jane, are you ready to face the gossip that will be broadcast about us? You seem so unbothered by this. Is there some thing more here that I should know?"

"No, my dear, it's simply not important to the people we respect and let the others think what they may!"

Frowning and staring at his confident wife, Harold let the matter drop. Whatever needed to be done, he would see to it.

***

By Christmas, the baby was crawling, and babbling and once she really began to walk and talk, her Mistress, the young Miss Janie Fleming, insisted the baby spend most of her day in the nursery, so the two could play. The baby looked, spoke and acted like the slave owners. Because the laws had become so restrictive, Mrs. Fleming would not allow the slave child to be tutored with Mistress Fleming, no matter how much the little Mistress pleaded.

Cotillion

"Jane. Jane! Have you seen him?" Mrs. Jane Wellington Fleming was amused by her young friend. She admired her youthful exuberance.

"Calm yourself, Juliet. You'll cause yourself to perspire!"

The women were in the sitting room off the master bedroom enjoying the afternoon. Juliet, still in her teen years, befriended Jane Wellington Fleming during Jane's mother's illness. Juliet's parents suffered with lung problems, which often remanded them to their beds. The young girl, their only child, was at ease tending the sick. With support from their slaves, she nursed her parents, and became a help to Jane, who admired and looked out for young Juliet.

"Really, Jane, haven't you heard about the Cotillion? How can you be so calm? These past few winters have been such a bore and the influenza has done its worst. At last there's a reason to get fancied up and catch up on every bit of news."

Jane answered, "Seems you think I'm some foot loose belle. Juliet, you're talking to a grown woman with an ambitious, handsome husband, and a young one just spoiling to discover every mischief Lucifer has yet to invent! I suspect you are plotting here."

Smiling, Juliet replied, "You know me too well, like the big sister I never had."

"Your parents cannot escort you and you know they'll sanction you going to the dance with Harold and me."

"Jane, don't you ever listen to the slave's gossip? I'm praying we will all be going to Stratford Hall come Saturday, but Stratford has been coming to Fleming Plantation these past two summers."

Jane noticed, "Why, you're flushed Juliet. Who has turned your head?"

The women beamed at each other with the joy and ease of friends who have developed a sisterhood untainted by the rivalry of siblings.

"It's young Robert of course! According to Ma Molly, if one would be so naïve as to believe what any Negro says."

"Juliet, you'd best stay out of kitchen gossip. You'll be talking like the Negros!"

Juliet continued her explanation, "Robert's brother, William Henry, was supposed to be watching for a run away Negro the Admiral paid dearly for. Buchanan's overseer was such a prig, that Missus asked William Henry to report to Buchanan's overseer. Oh, what's his name? Rastus! Yes, they called him Rastus."

"I'm sure that's not the man's name. Your mother mentioned the admiral's overseer. His coldness even upset her...and the Negroes hate him."

"Jane, you're missing the point! Let me tell you the good part!" Juliet popped from the divan, her golden curls rebounding with each step as she moved towards Jane's chair. In a flurry of petticoat ruffles, she knelt at her friend's feet. Neither pinching nor arsenic could have made her cheeks flush more.

Excitedly Juliet went on, "Hush, Jane, and please listen! You think William Henry makes Mrs. Lee, the esteemed Ann Hill Carter, proud—she never raves about her beautiful girls like she dotes on those plain-faced boys—well, you should see young Robert now! Jane, he's a strapping gentleman—and can he sit a steed!"

"For shame, Juliet, you sound like you've not only been listening to rumors, why you've been spying! Steed, that's such a military word. There's something scandalous about that look in your eye!"

They both giggled, using their delicate hands to cover their full-faced smiles. From the nursery room down the hall a toddler's loud pleas disturbed the women's chatter.

"Momma, Momma!" wailed the little girl. "No nap, Skokie, no! Please, Momma!"

Skokien stood in the chamber doorway. She was as comfortable in this ornate room as if it were her own. It was she who combined the prints and lace, ruffles and comforters to complement the seasons. Skokien's duties had doubled, and her skills increased as she matured. It was not difficult to please Jane Wellington Fleming. During several harsh winters, Jane Wellington Fleming's mother recuperated at the Manor. Influenza struck with a vengeance throughout the South. The old slaves often told Skokien about their harsher life in Baltimore and their trips to the "country" helping Mrs. Wellington's young married daughter, Jane, set up a country manor house. When the old woman died, they became permanent residents with the young couple, Harold and Jane Fleming.

In her job as nursemaid, Skokien sometimes felt weary. Little Janie was a bright child yet willful.

"Skokien," Mrs. Fleming pleaded, "do be patient with her. With the Almighty's help, she'll soon tire. Is Sophie in the kitchen? Bid her help you get Janie off to sleep. She has a way with her when she's irritable like this."

"She nearly smothers the child!" Juliet interjected. "It's probably that infernal singing." Juliet rose and left the two women to deal with the child. She stared out of the window, attempting to hide her irritation.

"Miss Juliet and I are visiting, Janie. Skokie will take you to the kitchen. Perhaps Sophie has a cookie and some milk for you there."

The child, sensing a victory, grabbed Skokien's hand and led her quickly away. Juliet, now pale and pouting placed both hands on her trim hips and complained.

"You spoil that child! You haven't heard half of my news and it's near time for tea. Aren't you even a little interested in the cotillion? Will you and Harold be attending? I've never known you to stay away from a ball. I need you to help me."

With both hands still on her hips, Juliet raised her voice. "I tried to tell you. Robert comes here! I don't know how his brother got him to do the admiral's bidding, but you can properly introduce us. I won't be going to the ball with mother and father this year. Surely, they'll approve of Robert. Jane, help me!"

Jane caught a bit of Juliet's excitement and wondered if she could interest Harold in attending. The friends set about devising a plan, while laying out frocks on the bed. They were oblivious to the familiar singing coming from the kitchen stairwell. Sophie was teaching Skokien her most soothing melodies. The smell of cookies announced time for tea.

At the Cotillion

A dozen carriages lined in a row at the south door of the Stratford Hall Plantation. The guests carefully mounted the steps to the second floor to enter the Great Hall. Thomas Lee, the builder of the gracious building did himself proud. The giant, ornate chandelier lit the entire room, giving those awaiting a parade of silhouettes in grand costumes vanishing into the waiting hall. The

30

east and west doors, great windows, and the north and south doors gave ample breeze even on hot summer evenings. With the heat of the day waning, the guests were most comfortable, even as the doors were closed to wend away the moths, beetles, and mosquitoes wishing to join the festivities.

The ladies were sipping cool minted sweet-tea in crystal tumblers and admiring the flurry of women's gowns being flaunted as they all waited for the return of the musicians.

Young Dan Crapster, in his well-tailored, gray satin suit approached Juliet and Jane. "Evenin' Ladies. You' all look mighty pretty tonight. Why, Miss Meriwether, you're a mirror likeness of your mother. Sorry to hear of her infirmity. How's she fairing these days?"

"Mother requires a great deal of care. We are thankful to God that she survived."

"And your mother, Mrs. Fleming, how is she fairing?"

Jane summoned her Sabbath face in order not to show her disdain. "The influenza took mother from us. Her servants did their best to keep her from suffering."

"Well I declare, we southerners have niggers, and you Flemins' have servants?" His boisterous laughter informed Jane that her effort to be civil had failed. His dismissal of her sad news justified her loathing of the young man and his father!

Dan's father was one of the "committee" that assailed her many winters before the fever ravaged Maryland. Juliet stood motionless as the two stared at each other with bold angry eyes. Juliet broke the tension with a feigned cough.

"I must say we would all welcome a cool breeze about now. Jane, please join me. I'm going to the provisions table. I think the fiddlers will be coming back soon. It will be wise to cool down while we can."

Not waiting for Jane to respond, Juliet took her by the arm and guided her away from Dan. Neither of the two stopped their glare until the ladies went out of the large glass doors where they enjoyed the breeze and refreshments.

"Why, Miss Jane Wellington Fleming, whatever is going on between you two? I've never seen you so livid. Your politeness brought me to surmise you'd taken a liking to Dan!"

"Liking! Those Crapsters came to our home leading a committee of slave catchers, dogs, chains, whips. They near maimed old Moses. I answered the door that Friday evening. The pounding and baying were so frightening, our servants were terrified!" I never told Harold the whole story. He would have confronted them and gotten himself shot. They were intent on doing harm."

***

Jane Wellington Fleming had summoned all her strength before she opened the door that wretched night.

Mr. Crapster, the spokesman greeted her. "Mrs. Fleming, we came to speak with the colonel about this looming situation with harboring runaways!"

Jane quickly, surmised their true agenda. Crapster pretended politeness and asked,

"Will the colonel be here this evening? We feel it necessary to inform you' all." The committee of men, their neighbors, knew Harold would not be home until the weekend.

"We wouldn't want to intrude on the Sabbath and

this is a pressing matter. There's a brazen nigger called Day Gal, she calls husself, Falashaday. She's been skulking around across miles of plantation. Hounds run her into the swamps, but this past evening, the hounds brought us right 'chere to yore bahn, before losin' the trail at the basin. Now this is one mean nigger an' she carryin' a chile. There's a fair reward for her return—dead or alive!" Crapster spoke firmly, scrutinizing Jane Fleming, searching for any sign of fluster to confirm his suspicion.

"I heard a commotion and sent my boy, Moses to secure the barn. I'm sure no runaway could get in. My darkies are fearful of the night and only the old ones stay in the quarters at night. We only have a half dozen and two sleep here in the garret. Your men saw Moses, taunted him edging your horses onto his feet and holding him at bay with your muskets. You near frightened him to death! Mr. Crapster you forced Moses to unlock the barn! Your inspection proved no runaways were there and you certainly ravaged all the sheds and shanties, spreading terror with your torches and muskets." She paused and stared full into his frowning face and narrowed eyes. "Are you here to search the Manor?" His wizened face stared back at her with gloating eyes of victory. She knew he had no intention of giving her an option.

"You *will not* threaten nor whip one soul on these premises! Do I make myself clear, Mr. Crapster? You will come with me from garret to root cellar, speak civilly to my chattel, and leave here satisfied that Flemings do not harbor runaways nor steal the property of others!"

Jane did not raise her stern voice, nor move nor blink, until she heard Crapster's muted, "Yessum'."

She turned, guiding her full petty coated gown skillfully through the living area to the root cellar and finally to the garret. Once alighted from the grand staircase to the narrow garret steps, she quietly announced,

"Sophie? Tilley? Mr. Crapster is here looking for lost property. You must show him due respect. He will not harm you nor defile your quarters."

The women stood as their mistress and the spokesman entered. The women shielded their nightwear with their hands. Their backs and heads bowed as they pressed against the low, sloping ceiling beams. Crapster narrowed his eyes, the lids lowered like a snake's, glowering at the wide-eyed women. A small window divided the space in half and barely allowed enough air for them to breathe. There were neither dressers nor cupboards— just a basket with folded clothing and a stool that supported a candlestick, the flame motionless in the stifling, quiet night air. He used his cane, ornately carved with a horse's head with bulging eyes, to poke into the basket and strike at the sleeping mats that were spread on opposite sides of the tiny room. The women fixed their gaze on their Mistress. They had never seen such sternness in her face or fire in her eyes. Those eyes never left Crapster. He did not meet her eyes. As he turned, he gave one more vicious thump on the clothesbasket and stomped down the tiny stairwell filling it with his out spread arms. He turned again onto the grand staircase, his free hand securely holding onto its shiny balustrade. At the bottom, he stepped aside allowing her to precede him to the front door. She held it as he led his awaiting committee into the enveloping darkness. Sophie and Tilley up on the garret steps, heard her pound her fist into the palm of her hand, speaking vehemently to the absent men.

"You bastards! You lying, sneaky bastards! How dare you come here feigning concern?" Suddenly aware that she'd given voice to her rage, she walked to the stairwell. "You've not heard a word of that vile talk and you'll not share one bit of this intrusion with Master Harold when he arrives tomorrow! Not a word!"

In chorus, the attic voices assured her, "No Missus, not a word." It was nervous, stifled laughter Jane heard from the upper room, yet it allowed her to relax and reflect on the evening.

***

At the Cotillion, Harold abandoned his conversation with his old military comrades. He never enjoyed the dancing. He would come at Jane's insistence, but always engaged in lively political talk with the men. Harold noticed Crapster's interaction and saw Jane's sober expression. He didn't fully comprehend why Jane despised the man but his instincts led him to follow the women over to the refreshment tables.

"Was that mutton-head Crapster bothering you? He only blathers about secession and fear of slave uprisings. Has he offended you ladies?" His wife beamed a welcome smile at her observant partner and reassured him that she had bid good riddance to young Crapster and his pretentious conversation.

"He likes to act the gentleman with his shallow inquiries about Mother's health. He's never met Mother and I expect he was speculating that she took ill with so many of the elders who suffered with last winter's plague. I do believe both his parents were made invalid by it. That's why others are doing the old gent's bidding.

Harold my dear are you acquainted with young Robert Lee?"

"Why, we rarely see him since his father died. I do know he is quite the young man now: recently graduated from West Point, second in his class! He's assigned here in Virginia, Hampton Rhodes I believe."

"Well our Miss Juliet seems to think he is here at Stratford."

Harold looked about the ballroom, with its yellow glow of the candelabras and bobbing shadows of the dancers. The musicians had returned and Harold had to raise his voice to reply.

"Now that could be the major general's son." He gave due respect to Robert's father, despite the man's fall from prominence. "Over there, in dress uniform. The Lee family has managed through these years to maintain their pride. They still spend holidays and summers here at Stratford. Of course, Robert was born here, but they have lived in Alexandria since the major general's demise."

There were so many ladies and young officers surrounding Robert that Juliet could not locate him and interrupted. "Where? Harold, where do you see him? Please point him out again."

"Why, Miss Juliet, are you wont to join that bevy?" Mrs. Fleming took delight in watching Harold tease Juliet, knowing he would eventually introduce her if she pleaded with him. Juliet was an expert at pleading and getting her way.

The three of them made their way around the skirt of the hall. Most of the young people had joined in the dance. When they reached Robert, he was with another young officer. Their crisp uniforms attracted a few veteran soldiers, who addressed the young men with questions, wondering where the young warriors' loyalties lay.

"What do you think, boys, will you be seeing action soon if those Yanks continue to threaten our economy? Surely you've heard the talk of separation."

Young Bobby was the first to respond. "Sir, there is no doubt in my mind. I stand with Virginia. Whatever the governor decides is best for Virginia, that's where my loyalty will ever remain!" The women stood silent, politely deferring to the men's obvious interrogation. They used their proximity to make their own assessments of the young officers. One of the elder veterans recognized Harold and took the opportunity to "test" Harold's loyalties and educate the cluster of admirers who were audience to his exposition.

"Well, if it isn't the barrister from Baltimore! We don't see you much at the local meetings. There's great concern these days with all that's going on with the darkies. Harold, how can you leave your lovely wife for such long periods—alone with your niggers? Ah know you don't keep many, but they all need to be seasoned. Best you keep a tight reign or you'll be left with that old black smithy turned stable boy! These crazy niggers are running off more and more. Ah don't know what eva possesses them to think they can just let the crops rot in the ground, leave the animals untended."

Harold Fleming listened respectfully, nodding and appearing to heed the old soldier's advice. He found it best to keep his thoughts private at social events. If his wife's family had not willed them their slaves, Harold would hire indentured to help on the plantation.

The old veteran continued unaware of Harold's true feelings. "Why, Colonel Crapster had a boy run off leavin the cows gorged and braying all night! He's had to use ball and chain on alla his boys. You think your slaves too old to run? Think again! There's a demon female comin round these parts, stealin groups o' niggas, young and old alike!"

Young Dan asked, "What do you hear about the slave problems when you're down at the County seat? The government going to help us out with tighter laws, aren't they? If they don't do something right soon, we're all gonna hafta hire more overseers and do some seasoning these run aways won't forget!"

If the old Soldier who was lecturing him knew that Harold considered his small cluster of slaves a true "gift" from his in laws, the old gent would shun him, consider him a treacherous nigger lover, and inform every other plantation owner of the hazard in their midst.

The women remained politely quiet, and were relieved when the young officers offered to bring them cool beverages, which they accepted gracefully. The older men continued spouting their political fears and strong beliefs.

"It's a simple matter of economics," one of the young officers explained to the women. "Don't believe that nonsense that we are all in some kind of jeopardy if the slave revolts expand, we have to make examples of those foolish enough to consider such lunacy—draw and quarter them, reduce them to fat. We have the rope, the whip and the gun, if shackles and collars and dogs don't teach 'em!"

Young officer Bobby looked at his companion, Buford, trying to get him to notice how disturbing his comments were to the women. Finally he said, "Buford, these ladies came to dance, not listen to threats of war, slave politics and revolts!"

"Well listen Bobby, are you implying that this flap about limiting the expansion of slavery has no credence? Perhaps that was what they were thinking in Santo Domingo. Haiti really happened, sir." The men moved closer into a tight group to continue the now fiery conversation of the veterans.

Bobby Lee attempted to tame the fervor. "It's talk, Buford, just talk. Nothing is going to change. The economy is thriving across the county and in the new colonies. We're no longer limited to tobacco. Whitney's gin brought cotton all over: not just rice crops in the marshes and the bay areas. No need to fear the end of the grand old South."

Bobby knew the women felt a bit reassured by his calm, confident contribution to the discussion, even so, Jane and Juliet moved gracefully away to where the women were clustered and joined in the more amusing pastime of guessing which of the dapper lads were old Georgia boys, traveling to all the cotillions in search of suitable mates, and which were dandies, the Dahlonega new rich traders and miners "in costume." Some of the dandies were old Yazoo sops squandering their inheritance.

It was these special times when the slaves managed rare visits. Fathers saw sons who'd been sold away and had grown into young adulthood. They were now teamsters or postilions like their fathers. They too talked politics, family news, shared their interpretation of what was to come, who had run and who was caught.

Moses knew most of the men, and dared to meet with the female slaves who were mostly in the kitchens and only went out to pick fresh mint or into the ballroom to

39

replenish the party fare. Anne was one of the unfamiliar slaves who greeted Moses as he sat in the summer kitchen, enjoying the breeze off the bluff. Anne's relaxed, confident demeanor piqued his curiosity. He found himself interrogating her.

"Where all do you come from, chile? You acts like you been in this mansion all 'o yo life." She smiled; her easy smile made her beguiling.

"Why I been here many a time, an at most all the grand houses in these parts. My Masta be Mr. Washington Custas. Folks in these parts don't know, brother, but he and his Missus been teaching us peoples at Arlington to read and write. I know you won't be broadcasting what I has to tell you, but Missus Molly an Masta preparing us for the day of freedom so we be able to fend for our selves!"

"Well, well. I do declare. Tha'ss some bit o' news. I'm mighty proud to meet you, Missy Anne, mighty proud."

"When ever I be in these parts, we surely will meet again, Moses."

They did meet again, many times, at those special gatherings. It was Missy Anne from the Custas Plantation who gave Mary Jane news of her father and his growing family. Amidst all the changes, Moses knew the old guard had not changed a bit. He wondered if he himself could bear the future he was clearly envisioning. What if he had to chose leaving his beloved South to uncertainties in the North? How would loyal southerners wanting to keep their way of life manage if they were forced to change? What if war really came to the warm, familiar place he knew as home? Moses made a deliberate effort to learn all that he could from the Custas slave and others like her. He mimicked speaking like a southern gentleman and sought out those who could read to him and inform him of happenings. Many southern slaves deliberated on their escape to the north, never knowing what challenges that freedom would bring, or if they would get there alive.

The Fleming slaves were valued and tended like any dutiful offspring might look after an inheritance. Stewardship was important to Harold. He never considered "seasoning" his slaves with whippings and collars, or chains. He knew the old Soldier had suspicions about his youngest slave. At least sixteen years had past since he was accused of ignoring and turning a blind eye to the slave problems and possibly allowing his old slaves to give aid to run a way. He successfully sued one whippersnapper slave owner for slander. That ended the accusations but not the suspicion. Back in the ballroom, Harold gracefully moved the conversation by acquainting the parties. Juliet got her introduction and was impressed with Bobby Lee's proud, decisive stand. The men continued their political, speculative debates while enjoying strong drinks.

One old soldier kept the young men captive while he expounded on his predictions for the decade to come. "Why before this secession talk is done we're goin' to see war. This will all come to a head. Our president, only in this first term is talking war with Great Britain over the Alaskan border. He's already declared war with Mexico! We have a lot to gain and that man from Tennessee is willing to negotiate, buy, dispute and win. This nation is growing and you young stallions will see some real battles with victory in sight. Mark my words, disputed land in Texas and other territories will be a part of our nation."

It was near midnight before the flushed dancers, and debating men went out to the waiting carriages.

Chapter Four

Joining the Ancestors 1850

When asked how old he was, Moses would reply, "Kain't say, but I do recall happenings: when them French folk took they country an open up the prisons! I was a full-grown man then. As a chile, I recollect the promises of them Loyalist an how we won the war from England. Young men I knew then went off to England! Folks say when the war was lost some o' them men went to cane fields in the Caribbean."

Moses, who had been primary, surrogate parent to young Mary Jane Lee, began preparing her for the new order he could clearly foresee. Skokien's baby girl had grown into a beautiful teenager. Her red hair and hazel eyes flashed with delight and mischief. She sprang about the manor in the same style of her mother: skirts and petticoats lumped aside so as not to trip dashing up and down stairs.

Moses and Mary Jane stood near the barn after finishing their tasks of feeding the chickens and fetching the eggs.

"You a young women now, same age I told an taught your mamma 'bout the world. She borned you, when she only 'bout your age, maybe fifteen, sixteen. She never had no momma could stay close an help her learn 'bout the world. This Flemin family ain't like most slave owners. Running was the onliest way us folks could ever consider being free an treated like children of God. Now you must plan how you be when you're free! Chile, I promise you, you going to see freedom! This talk about war, gonna be war! Those who done got their freedom: they helping all of us to be free. I know this in my bones! My sands most run out, my body be complainin' fierce. I come as close to freedom as I'll ever be, here right here on this plantation! I taught your momma how to tend the stock, harvest the crops, drive and ride the horses and use the whip, never give reason to get the lash. I watched her show you, all that she learned, and you shore one fast learner! When those ole hands come looking for women on the holidays, you momma only got grab one time, an she teach you fast how to hold on to yourself. When the right man come, you be the chooser. I seen that young man trying to court you."

Moses held Mary Jane's hands and smiled his approval. Mary Jane continued to gaze at her beloved mentor, trying to grasp all that he was now sharing.

"He all right, I give him my blessin'." Mosses sighed, and after a pause, stared at the grass under their feet and said, "I'm afraid he get himself done in, if he don't be very, very careful. His Masta going to sell him off, or chop off a piece of his foot, if he don't stop runnin'. And that man can read 'n write. That make him more dangerous. His Masta knows, readin' 'n writin', make him more likely be a free man 'for the war come!" They stood in silence for a spell, taking in the warmth and sweetness of the evening air.

"There is peoples near here an around the South, helping us get to the North—far, far North. You might not know how to read 'n write, but you can memorize all us ole ones know, an we knows plenty! And your young man—friend, George, he's like a wild stallion. He only know how to walk or run, no trottin', no canterin'. When they got him shackled, he walks away. When he files them off, he runs. He runs like a wild horse, they never ketch him! That man read 'n and write'n, he be gone. Gone 't the North Star." Moses gazed into the field. A proud look came over his face as though this young man was making his own dream come alive. Moses smiled right at Mary Jane, chuckling as he spoke, " 'Ole Moses next trip? I be goin' to marble town."

Mary Jane noticed how small Moses had become, how slowly he moved. His hair was nearly gone. Small puffs of white fuzz trimmed his scalp, just above his ears and in spots at the base of his skull. Serpentine scars on his neck stood in bold testimony of the harshness he had overcome. Mary Jane often gazed into the field, remembering Moses and fearing her George would meet his demise and be caught coming to the plantation through those abandoned tobacco fields.

***

The "run away" became a frequent visitor to the Fleming plantation. Much like young officer, Bobby Lee's visits to the quarters, he was also known yet "unnoticed" by all who knew his purpose.

Whenever war news, punitive slave laws, or uprisings happened, George, the run away, read disquieting details to those in the quarters.

"The sea is going be my way out, Mary Jane, and when I'm free, I'll send for you."

Moses and the runaway had often spent time together in those last years. Moses told Mary Jane, "Your George is one ole soul, he be thinkin' all the while 'bout makin' a life for you 'all in freedom. What I hear tells me he's going to do it—yassah, I calls him Ole George. He got more learnin' in that mine' o' his than he has years onna' this earth—more'n all of us together—and he listens too. Thass' a sign chile, a sign of an ole soul—like he been soppin up everthin' he seen an heard an plucks the best from all what's goin' on. Yassah, that's what I calls him, Ole George, and he smiles like he understands what's happenin' in this world, right now."

Proudly, Mary Jane affirmed Moses' belief and confidence in her chosen partner.

"Each time he runs, Moses, he sees more of the world. He's been to England this last time and he met white folks willin to help us: white and black fixin to help us to freedom. I trust him, Moses. I bless the Lord you two like each other. He'll be here on the holiday, my 'Ole George, he's bringing us more news about freedom."

In their silence, Moses smiles, recalling his last visit with George.

***

Moses and George the frequent visitor sat by the barn at the end of chores.

"Moses, I've seen wild horses running free on the shores in French waters. They run in herds and nobody bothers them. If folks come too close, they run quick as sunlight pops behind a cloud. In a shadow, they're gone. And you know Moses they're all white, every one, all white! They're white and free—what's that say to a black man?"

"No, no son. The Almighty fits a bein' to where they lives well. If'n it's pester flies, or safe hidin' from them what harm, their color protects 'em. Look at your skin, it's meant to protect from the sun—the sun we knowed 'fore we was stole to this place."

"You're a wise man, Moses. There's so much I'm trying to figure on. I've seen many ports and see the water as the way to freedom. There's a place called Cape Cod. A sailor, named Jonathan Walker, from up there set about making it his business to free slaves. Now he came down here to Florida and parts in the South in the winter of forty-four. When he was caught helping slaves they jailed him and they treat him like he's one of us. This judge, in a court of law, tethered him an branded him with a hot iron, like he's cattle, but he's out in the world, making good folks black and white, see the evil in this condition we're in![1] Other men at sea are helping us too, some of them white, placing them selves and their families in mortal danger."

Moses could never resist asking Ole George for a retelling of the Pearl.[2]

"George, tell 'bout that boat, *Pearl*—that happen right here on the Potomac."

"That's true, but they were found out an had 't face their masters, but they made the news and folks get more and more courage when they hear about the *Pearl* and that other Cape Cod sailor, turned abolitionist!"

---

[1]TownAlvin F. Oikle, The Man with the Branded Hand (Everett, MA 1998), 105-136.

[2] Dera Williams, post to AfriGeneas Books-Authors-Reviews Forum, "[History] The Pearl: A Failed Slave Escape on the Potomac," June 11, 2006, http://www.afrigeneas.com/forum-dex.cgi?md=read;id=1523

***

Moses was the oldest slave and the first of Mary Jane's surrogate family to join the ancestors. When Moses died, the women tried as hard as they could to have him rest. He fought death like he'd fought all his life. He gasped for air, clawed anyone attempting to moisten his lips or clear the mucus from his mouth and throat. They sat him up. They laid him down. He begged to be in the old soft chair they had salvaged from the big house, and at the very end he spoke a gibberish: sounds they had never heard before, a tongue he had long forgotten, from a mother he couldn't remember, from a land he'd never seen. They buried him right there on the plantation like he hoped. There was no "marble" marker, yet the shady north slope of the tobacco field was a truly dignified plot.

Moses fought but Ma Molly left them with grace. Before Ma Molly died, George knew she was ailing and had taken to her bed. Ma Molly was the most attentive to his news, since Moses passed.

Before Ma Molly's health began to fail hope danced in her eyes when he spoke. She would look at Mary Jane Lee, her woman child, and gloat. "Chile you goin' to be a free woman one day soon. I feels' it in my heart. Whenever that runaway comes around, tellin' o' all thass' happenin', I feels it."

It was Ma Molly who instigated the joining ceremony. "Before you be momma an poppa, less' have us a joinin' ceremony. He's havin' to run, duckin' 'n dodgin'. Them hounds goin' to get him caught. Ceremony gives yo' a poppa fo' yo' chillen'. His time bein' aroun' here being shorta' an sweeta'. Best we be makin' this a blessin'

48

whilst we can."

When Ma Molly's time came she spoke bravely. "Won't be long now, and I done' want to hear no moanin' 'n wailin' 'bout my passin'. It's my time, can't even feel any more pain in these old legs. They' floatin' off already."

She peered at the strained faces: Tillylish, trying to smile through her tears, and Dahl, frowning fierce enough to scare the reaper away. When Ma Molly looked Sophie in the eye, a loud blubbering wail flew out of Sophie's mouth and filled the room. Ma Molly and Tillylish had to cover their mouths to keep from laughing. Sophie took herself outside the cabin and began to sing, sing so loud the birds flew off in fright. Before the sun set, Ma Molly was sleeping with the ancestors.

Mary Jane often studied the rise behind the fallow tobacco field, where her George slipped onto the Fleming plantation after the evening meal when he would least likely be noticed. George was not at the burials. His last visit resulted in his recapture.

With the Flemings and the older slaves in Baltimore and Ma Molly and Moses gone, Mrs. Mary Jane Lee Washington confided in her childhood companion, Mistress Janie.

"They caught him, Mistress. Word has it he's been sold, in ball and chain. My poor George, we may never ever see each other again!" Both women held sadness in their eyes, yet shed no tears. This was the fate of runaways.

***

When Bobby Lee's military duties and assignments increased, his visits to the Fleming Plantation ended. Skokien had accepted the loss of her "visitor." Her last meeting with Bobby Lee was the unburdening of his heart.

"Life as we know it is slipping away, Skokie. This talk of separation and perhaps even war—it's serious talk. My military assignments will end our visits, but there are many changes yet to come. I've taken a wife. She's a spirited woman. She has her own servants, there's no likelihood you'll ever meet. I know you'd like each other. You and baby Mary Jane will be well cared for here with the Flemings. It's my understanding the Colonel and his wife will be spending most of their time in Baltimore. It's likely you'll be going with them. It's a beautiful city Skokien. You'll have a good life there. This whole matter of slavery is money talk. The real problem as I see it is saving our way of life!"

Skokien listened with little sadness. She saw how troubled her Bobby had become. It was as if he was being torn in two by the war talk.

"I done know what separation will mean for us here in Maryland, but you been praisin' Virginia and I's sure thas' as nice a place as Maryland. I can't 'magine the south goin' to pieces!"

Her innocence always made Bobby smile. He seemed pleased that she had feelings about their beloved south. When he left, she was certain his actions would be valorous and well thought out. He was truly a southern gentleman, doing what southern gentlemen were raised to do.

Chapter Five

Baltimore

Harold and Jane Wellington Fleming spent more time in Baltimore. Harold at first went alone, and then his wife accompanied him as they attended his parent's affairs and ultimately, their burials. The political climate was less tempestuous, less frightening to them both. There were fewer rumors, posses and raids.[1] The older Fleming homestead needed repair and maintenance. Mrs. Jane Wellington Fleming oversaw the details and brought Sophie and Skokien with her to do the heavy chores. Mary Jane, Dahl and Tillylish remained at the mansion in Frederick County. Mistress Janie Fleming became the mistress of the Manor House. The fields were no longer cultivated, the gardens served the table and fed the animals.

Skokien found herself living in Baltimore, where she found a community she never dreamed existed. She found it at the Bethel A.M.E. Church. She went every Sunday they were in Baltimore. Unable to write letters to her girl, she stored all her news for the next holiday or Sunday visit to the Manor House. She nearly burst holding her news, her discovery: an amazing event in church. She knew Mary Jane would be pleased. It all began with a conversation about her mother, Fallashiday.

---

[1]Visit Baltimore, "Black History Month & Baltimore's Black History," http://baltimore.org/multicultural/black-history

"Mornin', Sister. 'Fore I came here to Baltimore I thought I'd be lonesome, missin' my young-un'—she's now a woman—but dis here church is feelin' like my new home, with sisters 'n brothers."

Skokien and the woman she had come to know as Harriett would seek each other out after the long sermons. They often met in the church hall where dinner was served before folks went home.

Harriett returned the sentiment, "I feel much like that myself. I grew up not knowing my momma 'n poppa. Folks who raised me up was livin' here free in Baltimore. I got 'dropped' by a run away and only know what they tell me. I praise the Lord for my life here with those good peoples! Dis here church been a sanctuary for us folks. Dey tells me the folks here separated theyselves' from the white church back in 1784. Dere's lots of our peoples here be free peoples an' do they best dey can fo' all of us."

"Well bless ma' soul. I can be thankful to the Lord fo' my family, the white ones and the black. Dey sure took me in, and raise me up proppa too!"

"Chile' I know yo' name be Skokien, and mine be Harriett Freeman. Thass' a name ma people took fo' they selves. What yo' call yo self', Flemin?"

"Nobody tells me what to call maself. I'is juss' Flemin property. There's some kind o' caution 'bout knowin' too much 'bout my momma. Her takin' chances to come by 'n see I'm in good hans and they chasin' her evy-where' with hounds 'n muskets. Them bounty men call her Day Gal, but I knows her name be Fallashaday."

"I can't b'leave yo spoke ma momma's name, Fallashaday. My momma been running' fo' years, livin'in swamps, livin' wid Indians. Dey been wantin' to catch her, dead o' alive all dese years. As I know it, dey never did catch her, an' yo' her chile, my momma Fallashaday's chile? Good Lord have mercy!"

The women fell silent, listening to the clatter of dishes, as the tables were spread with platters of chicken, dumplings, greens, corn bread and biscuits and ham. The church service always included a social component with food, music and merriment, but neither woman took a bite of food. They stared right at each other in wide-eyed amazement.

Another churchwoman saw their stricken faces and came to inquire.

"Sisters,—yo' all right? Yo all' lookin' mighty poorly, like yo juss loss yo' bess frien 'o yo' Chile. Whass' wrong?"

The intrusion broke their spell and they began to smile through a quiet stream of tears.

They continued to stare and scrutinize each other then, burst into rapid chatter sharing every story they had ever heard about the infamous, Day Gal. Skokien felt somehow glad people who raised her had actually seen her mother, and they claimed when a baby, she had seen her too. Harriett Freeman was a younger woman with no memory of seeing her mother, but she remembered the stories, proudly. The women had found a deep meaning to their greeting. They were indeed, sisters. Their friendship became a bond where they committed to meeting outside of church.

The Baltimore Letters

At the Plantation in Frederick County, Mary Jane skillfully cared for the livestock. Moses had taught her husbandry skills and she took full charge even before his frailty limited him. Mail was exchanged regularly. Doting parents sent loving, newsy letters to their daughter. Inquiries and pleasantries were sent in return. Mary Jane would place the mail on Master Harold's big oak desk, purposely placing a bloom or fancy folded napkin nearby, so that Mistress Janie would notice its arrival. The women had become quite comfortable with the small household. The chores were lighter, some of the rooms were closed, no need to keep a fire going in the great hall.

The Fleming's friend and neighbor, Juliet became fond of Mistress Janie as she grew into adulthood. Janie's feisty nature now looked appealing to Juliet. She wrote to her friend, Mrs. Jane Fleming:

> *My Dear Friend Jane,*
> *What do you think of your Janie being my*
> *bride's maid? I dast not ask her before con-*
> *sulting you. If she is not interested, she*
> *will not hesitate to tell me.*

Jane Fleming responded:

> *Dear Friend Juliet,*
> *I am so happy for you, finding your true*
> *love. Your Charlie is as much a gentleman*
> *as Bobby Lee ever was and from a proud*
> *Maryland family. It is a special person who*
> *studies medicine and serves an entire com-*
> *munity as he does. And there he was right*
> *under your nose while caring for your par-*
> *ents!*
> *I would not hesitate to ask her, since she is*
> *determined to stay in Frederick to study.*

Juliet's next newsy letter revealed what Mrs. Fleming had already surmised.

> *Dear Friend Jane,*
> *Then you know she is learning midwifery?*
> *Janie was being coy about letting me know*
> *you all were aware. It eases my mind that*
> *you know. My Charlie acquainted her with*
> *the most experienced midwife he could*
> *find. Janie is doing the schooling then she*
> *will join the team and be licensed!*

The sadness in Harold's eyes rarely left his countenance. He grieved when his beloved Janie insisted on learning midwifery. In his letters he argued:

> *Dearest Janie,*
> *It is not safe, traveling about the county*
> *with a married man, even if he is a medical*
> *doctor. It simply is not wise! He often trav-*
> *els with a mulatto midwife. No respectable*
> *woman should risk her safety in such com-*
> *pany.*

After the excitement of Juliet's wedding, life resumed its ordinary ways. The letter exchanges continued. If it hadn't been for Mary Jane's newly discovered "condition," one might consider life at the Manor had become a bit lonesome or downright boring. Both Jane and Harold met the news with surprise, and a dollop of fear that was not spoken aloud.

***

It was nearly the end of winter in 1852 when the mail came to Harold and his wife in Baltimore. The latest letter included news of their youngest slave being with child. Harold deduced that the Sunday Revival Meeting brought more than the word of God to their Mary Jane. This alarmed him, but he was certain his wife held secret pleasure in the news as she could hardly wait to get back home when she knew it was time for the birth. He could only wonder how often the elusive runaway was on the plantation, unnoticed by all, or at least, unnoticed by him and his zealous neighbors. Harold wondered if this slave was still alive, crafty enough to return. He'd heard of slaves risking life and limb to keep contact with their loved ones. He prayed no evil come of this news, this news that gladdened the hearts of his wife and daughter.

Harold had come to worry a great deal about all matters happening in the turbulent social climate. He confided in his wife. "I've managed to allow those who chose to believe our Araminta, Mary Jane, is of my seed. That mistruth allows those separatist to half respect me, but there's talk again of us harboring runaways. My dear Jane, please tell me it's not true. The codes are so vile now: we can lose everything, not just reputation. I've seen the results of these militias. Even plantation owners are shown no mercy at their hands!"

"Harold, dear, we are not 'harboring,' but there is a young man who frequents the quarters. Moses kept good watch and knew these parts like a fox. It's a pity Mary Jane cannot have what our other loyal servants dream about, just having a family, choosing their own partners. Would you consider manumission, Harold?"

"Why, Jane Wellington Fleming! You know a great deal more of this than you're admitting. What all do I need to be prepared to deal with? Do you have any idea the danger you're flirting with here?" Harold's hair had turned silvery and his once ruddy complexion, sallow with age. Now his pale face flushed red with stifled rage, his kind eyes filled with fear.

"I know it's not the bounty you wish for when you speak of manumission. Be truthful here wife. Leave nothing out!"

Jane skipped the details of the revival held on their back acre, the day George Washington and Mary Jane Lee had their ceremony. Moses had kept watch for vigilantes.

Slaves from all the neighboring plantations had come to hear the traveling preacher. He brought his own tent and the men erected it under a clump of shade trees. Sunday was the day slaves had been allowed to gather. Traveling men and women of God preached and prayed and spread the word. Children got to see their parents, brothers and sisters from within traveling distance, gathered in the woods, sang lustily and exchanged whatever good and bad news they held in their hearts until they could meet again.

Now a woman, young Mistress Janie Fleming knew her play pal of yesterday had taken a husband in the tent in the woods. She and her mother had turned a blind eye to the extra cooking and fussing in the summer kitchen. There was such a celebration, so many wagons, and an unknown preacher; a vigilance committee formed that night to investigate. The ordinance Harold was informed of in Baltimore resulted from just such an event. No runaways were caught, but suspicions were raised, and Harold Fleming's neighbors were frightened.

There would be no more traveling Negro preachers

allowed in Frederick County. No more evangelists, no more tents in the woods. Any such gathering and those participating would be publicly tortured, burned, boiled or hung: whatever the posse felt would best teach slaves a good lesson.

Harold's worst fears were quickly mounting. Mrs. Jane Fleming had been sitting embroidering in the great hall where Harold took his after dinner nap, just as they were that Sunday. Neither of them had heard the joyful singing nor the Committee's horses that particular evening. Mistress Janie had met the men and later reported the details to her mother.

Mrs. Fleming slowly gave Harold every detail she thought prudent to share. "Revival meetings may make folks anxious, but there was no trouble, Harold. Perhaps the Committee feels such large religious gatherings might be a problem in the future. Why, Harold, you were here at home that Sunday. There was no problem, no talk of runaways. I hear the Committee went into the gathering to ease their minds."

The less Harold knew the better for their safety. He could never tell a false hood without bodily giving himself away. Embarrassment shone on him like glowing coals: red face, stammering, he would retreat into silence. As a barrister, he could never defend an evil cause or a guilty party. He would abstain; refer the cause or the case to his colleagues. His litigation dealt exclusively with land issues and property rights. He was known to be fair, and honest men sought him out.

He stared at his wife, managed to take one deep breath, and left the room.

Baby George

The Flemings returned to the County each spring. The orchards were in full bloom, peach and cherry blooms fluttering their petals on the breeze. Letters could not hold all the joy expressed in their greetings with one another. Skokien, bubbling with blessings greeted her grandson. "Yo mamma be mighty proud 'o you Chile, yo pappy too. Bright eyes lookin' right hat me wonnerin', who dis white haired scrawny womans takin me from my momma's arms? Well lemme tell yo. Ize yo' granma!"

Mary Jane scurried to bring the luggage and parcels from the coach and set them in their proper places. She was in full charge at the mansion. The great hall was aired and prepared for the family. A light meal awaited them in the dining room. When she left to tend the horses, baby George remained in his grandmother's arms. He studied the new faces while listening for his mother's familiar voice. The women continued exchanging information in between the hugs and kisses whirling about the room.

When the elder Flemings and their daughter enjoyed their repast in the dining hall, the servants retreated to the kitchen where a fresh burst of noisy, joyful news was exchanged.

"Momma, my George been here an run again. Last time he run, got the ball and chain and was sole' down South Carolina. He been writin' letters to Baltimore, to Masta. Miss Janie reads Masta's notes 'bout George's messages he sens' to Baltimore. Thass' how I know he' safe right now." Solemnly, Mary Jane continued, "Don't matter how much I tell him, 'don't take too many chances, comin' here, they' goin' to catch you and do you bad harm.' Moses always tryin' to calm me, sayin' his Ole George gonna be safe and free too! Maybe Moses right. I pray he'safe every night'n day. Momma you say you an yo' newfoun' sista' been spendin' Sundays together? When will I get to meet this Aunt Harriett?"

Sophie, Dahl and Tillylish halted their simultaneous chatter to hear more about the newfound child of Fallashaday. Skokien explained, "Chile, she' a free woman. She'plannin' to visit here on the Independence Holiday. She work' fo' a family as nursemaid an' cook, askin' to have some days to husself in July. You' meets' her den. When I see them letters comin' and goin' here, I be writin' messages in ma head to tell yo' alla the things goin' on in Baltimore."

Sophie chimed in to fill in details about the shops in Baltimore and the mixing of free and slave black folks. Dahl had been vying with Tillylish to hold baby George. Without words, Dahl's rare broad smile won over as Tillylish handed the sleeping baby over and huddled closer to the table to hear the details about the markets and magic of the city. When the baby awakened and announced his hunger, all conversation paused as the admiring female clutch watched their grown Mary Jane suckle her first baby.

***

The years passed quickly. Harold made peace with his headstrong daughter. It was Juliet who eased both parent's minds. She wrote:

Dear Friend Jane,
All is well here. Now that Janie has fin-
ished her formal training, I've arranged for

my postilion, Max to accompany my hus-
band on all calls outside of Frederick. Max
knows all the roads and trails of Maryland
and Virginia. I pray you will approve of
Janie traveling with Charlie when the time
comes for her to gain practical experience.
Janie told me of your anxiety.
You may be pleased to know that I too will
travel with the old midwife and my hus-
band, as weather conditions allow. My life
now overflows with goodness and purpose.
I see how this training has given your
Janie a similar feeling.

The south lumbered along, desperately trying to hold onto its customs and economy. In the north a particular fomentation was brewing. The populous became polarized about the slavery issue. The topic dominated printed material and conversation. Harriett Beecher Stowe's novel *Uncle Tom's Cabin* fueled passions. Unimagined circumstances came to pass. A black man, John Parker, walked freely in the middle of the street in Riply, Ohio, carrying a gun. Parker was a known runaway, sought dead or alive by bounty hunters; he remained a free man. Groups of northern black women, some free some slave, some runaways, organized and attacked bounty hunters freeing the captured.[2] Fear and anxiety affected northerners and southerners alike. Things became more precarious for run aways.

---

[2]The Life of William Parker and His Impact on the Christiana Riot
http://muweb.millersville.edu/~ugrr/christiana/Parker.html   page 4 of 10

George Buchanan Washington (The Elder)
in Hyannisport, MA

Chapter Six

'Ole George

George stood alone on the ship's deck looking out at the city of Boston. He spoke to himself, "This cold place looks like a picture book, those tall sheds and big wharf, nothing like home. No bayou anywhere. No wonder the birds go 'way from this place. When this hitch is over, I'll be lookin' to find some place for all of us, place so far north Crapster freeze like a' icicle. Mmmmm huh!"

George Washington's wry smile fades slowly back to his usual sober countenance. Even when George was a boy, it was hard to rile him. His dark face had nary a wrinkle, yet his tightly curled hair had already turned grey. It was neither short nor wooly as it appeared. In his youth that mat of hair had surprised a few southern gentlemen who stroked it for good luck, only to find their hands nearly bruised by the harsh steely texture of the dense coils. He continued to speak aloud, with no one listening.

"Goin' home is not goin' t' happen. Ain't even safe 't go ashore up in these parts. Our young 'uns will have to depend on Missus Flemin's good heart and my Mary Jane from now on, 'til Missus make good her promise." He paused, staring out at the empty wharf. His train of thought continued, filling the silence with his observations.

"Dogs everywhere, bounty dollars goin' higher, everybody and anybody turn you over. Ole Crapster going to take my leg next, then this 'ole George won't be no use to no ship. The sea is so still and quiet, and no moon. Sure makes a-body want to steal home. This big water so powerful. I declare, it give' me power, like takin' on the first president's name. Ain't nobody tangle with George Washington no more."

In the quiet and peace of his lonely thinking, George made commitments to himself. He vowed no one would ever call him George Buchanan. There was just one good thing he recalled that came from Buchanan Plantation: book learning with Frankie. George made a promise to put that learning to use each day for the rest of his life. He could think of nothing worse than getting sold again, from one bad plantation like Crapster's to another.

George considered he was seeing some bad times: talk of war, black folks begging in the streets in Boston City. He wondered how many could find the will power to get all their family and friends up to the North Star. Such thoughts made him feel low as he realized his work mates would be gone 'til daybreak. He decided to do some hauling or setting down plans for Mary Jane. He sighed wearily as he thought about his Mary Jane, believing she was the bravest soul he'd ever seen, and he'd seen plenty.

The sailors returned from their excursion on shore. The sound of their many feet scurrying on board brought George out of his reverie. A half dozen dark men alighted the gang plank like gazelles being hunted by lions. Their bright eyes shone even in the darkness. They hailed George as they streamed across the deck.

One of the sailors ran by panting, waving his hat at George and told him, "Them streets is crawlin with bounty hunters. They's hand bills on every post. Injin Joe here, heard the men in the saloon, drunk as they wuz, fixin to lay hands on one 'o us, juss to see how much they could git!"

Most of the men went down below, but Joe stood quietly beside George. The silence was comfortable. When George turned to go below, Joe asked the question. "You one 'o them run-aways, right? New law says you have to go back to who owns you, no matter if you' in Massachusetts, it's just like being in the south. Bad law."

George knew Joe was a free Indian from Cape Cod. The men had been on several long voyages together. Black and Indian sailors were called Black Jacks and it was a fair guess that many of the black men were either runaways, or freed by the British when they served in the Revolution.

George could see the night's event had stirred up Joe's curiosity. "Well, you' lookin' at a free man right now. I planned to buy my freedom from a bad master. He took me for a fool, kept increasin' the price so as I'd never be able to save enough!"

Joe stared at George, sizing him up and down. "You got gray hairs on your head, but you a young man. I seen how easy you haul an climb. How long you been free?"

George was enjoying Joe's company and allowed himself to laugh at the irony of his so called freedom. "Far as I can tell, I was born in October, 1813, in Howard County, Maryland. I've had several masters, Ben Crapster being the first an the last! Got sold on the block when I was seventeen, for six hundred dollars. Buchanan owned me before I ran. Got sold off to Fredericksburg County to work on a farm and ran away again to Baltimore where I shipped out to England, stayed at sea two years, landing in South Carolina.

65

That's when I got hauled back to the old plantation, Howard County, Maryland, in ball and chain. I lived there three years and married a slave girl on the next plantation."[1]

Joe asked, "How'd your master think you could buy yourself?"

"Oh that's the good part. He knew I leaned to read 'n write and been all over the world and had some money owed me from my last ship, wasn't given leave to get it. That ship was in Maryland harbor and I devised a plan to let my master believe I could get all of the money he was asking for in one day, if he let me get to Baltimore. He, taking no chances, I'm with the ball 'n chain, given just enough time to get there 'n back. I hid in the swamps 'til I got them off: no dogs scent you in the swamps. Once they were off, I became a free man, worked my way north never stopping 'til I reach St. John, New Brunswick!"

Both men were smiling broadly as George proudly ended his story. George added, "All this evenin' I been figurin' how to get my wife an children to freedom. I expect fore this coming summer is over they'll be here with me."

"You plan to buy her?"

"No. Her missus goin' to give her freedom papers. She'll have to come by the railroad so she don't get kidnapped and sold deep-south, like those jackals in the saloon been plottin'. That's happenin' everywhere these days."[2]

---

[1]Buchanan is reportedly Old George's first and last master.
[2]Caroline Washington Pocknett, written account of newspaper interview of George Washington, c.1910.

The End of the Quiet Times

Communication flowed regularly from the Plantation to Baltimore. Harold was relieved and impressed when mail came from Boston. Over the next six years he was able to tell Mary Jane that letters were now coming regularly from her husband. Politics and domestic issues mellowed; it wasn't until 1858 that tensions again began to rise.

Mistress Janie read the part of her father's letter meant to inform Mary Jane. "I'm sorry to tell Mary Jane that her husband George's sister Henrietta was recently sold. He has implored me to take note of her new circumstance so that he might find her. So many slaves being sold: every day looks like a funeral, watching the darkies in Baltimore. Sorry to be the bearer of sad news, but there is good news also. Your young man has found work. Right now he is in Boston, Massachusetts." Mistress Jane Fleming finished reading and placed the mail back on the desk.

Mary Jane did not find the news startling. She calmly added her comment. "I's so thankful he' safe. I never met his sister. He 'tole me she never would travel North with him since they were old enough to run, no matter how he pleaded with her. Surely she regrets her choice. It seems men fair better than women when they run to freedom."

The women retreated to the parlor off the dining hall. As the slaves left to continue the chores Mistress Janie Fleming watched the young slave, wondering how often Mary Jane had made the same decision this woman Henrietta made. Mistress Janie called to the young slave as they left, stating, "You'll never have to fear being sold. Mother and father have made the decision to follow the law and secure freedom papers for you and the children."

***

It wasn't until the group had come from Baltimore and Mary Jane shared the manumission news with her mother, Skokien, that she was able to show any emotion. It was Skokien who whooped aloud, running to her daughter, shouting. "Ah knows it was gonna happen. Hallelujah, thank you, Jesus! This been on ma' mine since ole George come aroun an yo'now bein' a momma an the Poppa bein' gone way north."

Mother and daughter embraced. Mary Jane's expression was difficult to read.

"Does this please you, Mary Jane?" Mrs. Fleming observed the joyous reunion and saw confused amazement in her youngest slave's eyes. "It's the only way you can safely join the father of your children. There is no longer any safety in him coming here. Master Harold has papers for you. When you're ready to travel, we will make certain they are safely on your person."

***

Sights and sounds in Baltimore affected everyone. Harold watched the legal system fill with slave codes, harsh, restrictive, and inhumane. Lynching increased in manner and numbers: drawing, quartering, burning, maiming. Even the hangings became spectacles of humiliation, disemboweling, cutting off genitals while the slaves were not yet dead. Some outlaw vigilante groups were made up of lawmen. It made him ill.

It was the spring of 1856. Harold was seated in the

small parlor off the dining room opening the mail. He addressed his wife. "My dear, since the uprisings, folks have gone near mad with revenge. The opposition to slavery is as fierce as these rogue vigilance committees. Horrible things are going on and the laws are not helping matters. It's time. I do not want Mary Jane's husband skulking around the Plantation."

"Harold, I know it's been a long time that we made the decision not to sell our slaves. Buying and selling for this reason or that is still going on. Father and son have disowned each other, just due to their opposing feelings about owning slaves. The Rowdown Plantation taught us all a lesson. Major Bragdon could never have anticipated the tension and death his family endured. Runaways murdering their owners!"[3]

"We can still act within the laws as they now stand. The slave pens are filled each week. Maryland families are quickly selling off their slave holdings. Judge Ezra Michael has put my mind at ease. His friend and colleague, Judge Ephraim Cutler supports my thinking about manumission.[4] I've been entrusted with a confidence, which I dare not share. These are fine southern gentlemen, old family. We must act now!"

Jane interrupted, "With this war looming, there is no assurance of safety, with or without legal papers. I know the time has come, but I have little confidence that common sense prevails. It seems not to matter if a

[3]The Life of William Parker and His Impact on the Christiana Riot," Millersville University, http://muweb.millersville.edu/~ugrr/christiana/parker.html

[4]Links to the Past, " Beginning of the Underground Railroad across Southeast Ohio," http://henryburke1010.tripod.com/id14.html

slave is free or runaway. All reason seems lost to profit, risk and evil!"

This same spring of 1856, the Flemings had come from Baltimore to the Plantation in Frederick County. It had become their custom to enjoy the sights and smells of the country side coming into full bloom, bursting with color and wild life. They found a special comfort returning to these old familiar surroundings, and the servants were overjoyed to be together, as they opened the house for summer.

The couple sat in the small drawing room reading newspapers and a small collection of postal notices. Harold finished reading the news paper and held a letter from Old George in his hand. His thoughts were still with the news. He mused, wondering how Representative Preston Brooks could enter the chamber and attack Senator Charles Sumner with a metal cane, and beat the man unconscious. He could not believe Brooks beat Sumner about the head, bloodied him to where he had to be carried away. All this violence and rancor about slavery, and speeches on abolition, now even the Senate had gone mad!

He paled at the thought of how intensified, ruthless and polarized folks had become. His wife noticed the despair and tension in his expression. With trembling voice she asked, "Is it bad news? Has Mary Jane's George sent us bad news?"

Harold quickly composed himself, handed her the letter inviting her to see for herself that it did not contain bad news. He placed the newspaper article under the wool throw on his lap. He chose to keep such violent reports to himself.

In the 1856 election, the Republican candidate was

John C. Freemont, the American candidate was President Fillmore, and the Democrats nominated James Buchanan, who won. The slavery issue raged on. Before Buchanan's term ended, seven states seceded from the Union. The Flemings agonized at the political climate. They had decided to delay Mary Jane's journey as she was pregnant. They wondered if it was too late, too dangerous to follow through on their promise to their youngest slave.

Mrs. Fleming asked, "Harold what can we do?"

Harold was surprised to hear the angst in his wife's voice. He felt quite alone with these matters. "Dear wife, you have so many times reassured me. Trust me Jane. We will take no chances with our Mary Jane. She will travel a safe path, through Pleasant View, the negro village near the Episcopal Church. That farm area is safe. From Cumberland, she'll get to the Potomac. The judge and I have contacted people there who will help purchase transport tickets and safe lodgings. Nothing will be left to chance. If there is any sign of difficulty, they will move from Ohio to Lake Eerie into Canada. Her George has written names of contacts that Mary Jane can take with her. I have respect for that young man. I've recently learned he not only reads and writes English he's fluent in French and Spanish!"

The Journey

It was 1859 when the last letter came. Little George had his sixth birthday and baby brother James had joined the Washington family.

"Sophie, we are leavin' on the Sabbath! Masta' Flemin has all manner of papers. Down river, it ain't even legal no more to give slaves freedom papers. George is goin' to

71

meet us, somewhere, somewhere between Boston and Canada."

Sophie just watched Mary Jane pace up and down the stone floor of the summer kitchen, clasping her hands tightly together. "I never know what I feel most. They's such excitement in me, but most times it just feels like fear. The worst kind of fear: a' feared it won't happen an a'feared it will! Maybe it's just a plan, some idea, a story 'bout someone else. Oh Sophie what if we get lost? They say I must walk Injun trails, get on boats 'n wagons, for days on end!"

Sophie smiled as Mary Jane paced. "Chile you can't b'leave all o' those tales, 'bout people bein' snatched in Baltimore and walkin' trails. Yo' got helpers all d' way to d' North. Dey's a woman near dese parts been bringin' whole families to Canada. Dere's a lot o' folk, free, black 'n white helpin'. Dey get yo' to where t' go next. Juss' listen close an' follow what dey say. Yo' got a good mine 'n yo' chillen be listenin' good and wone' be no trouble a' tall. Yo' George sendin' all yo' needs to remember, an' money too, fo boats an' coaches. He been comin' here safe in summer 'an 'winner and fall. Just do like he say an' yo' be 'juss fine!"

Mary Jane looked down the path and saw her first-born George, bringing a bucket of fresh water for cooking. He was a lean, sturdy six year old. "Sophie, look at him. He' so young, too young t' have so much on him. I can hardly bear to think how long it will be 'fore I see him! He was so open to the plan, so ready to help and stay behind. My heart's bustin' with pride 'n fear, 'n excitement. It's too much just too much feelin' t' hold in my heart. I think I'll die before this journey ever begins!"

Little George was smiling as he turned into the

kitchen. His thoughts were as full of feeling as his mother's. He reviewed what he had been told: Mother 'n Jimsey be leaving this Sabbath. This gonna be some day! They got all they need to get to the North Star. I's glad I's stayin'on to help the Flemins'. Talk 'o war 'n things is changin' right here. I' be seein'whass' happen here. Papa sen' word to masta 'bout whass' happen up north. I' be right here helpin' Sophie. Thass' gonna be my job!

Mary Jane kissed him lightly on his cheek and took the bucket. She looked to the heavens, sighed so deeply she swooned. Quickly steadying herself, Mary Jane noticed Sophie beaming her feelings of pride and pleasure directly into the boy's eyes.

At the Manor house Mrs. Fleming packed carefully selected supplies into nap sacs: one to strap on Mary Jane's back, the other inside a grip with things for baby James. They gathered for the meal: little George and the slave women in the kitchen, the Flemings in the dining hall. The elder Flemings summoned Mary Jane into the drawing room, leaving the others to complete the chores.

"Your travel bags are ready," Harold declared, "and you and the missus will be securing your papers." With that announcement, he hurried out of the room.

"Mary Jane, we will be sewing your papers to your petticoat. We're taking no chances. Don't be alarmed, this is simply a precaution. Now let's get to work here, off with your petticoat. You will be traveling light, only one set of clothing, no changes." Mrs. Fleming and Mary Jane set about as a team, finishing in no time at all.

As they worked, Mrs. Fleming continued, "You will have adequate papers to travel, but if something unforeseen should happen, you have all the documents to prove you're free."

Attending to a task, relaxed Mary Jane. She began to feel ready. This was no dream. They left at dawn. Mary Jane held secret the fluttering she could now feel in her womb. The journey was long and arduous and her little Jimsey was a trooper: toddling along pathways and sleeping through nights as if he were in his own bed. She met Quakers who asked her if she "ken" what she was instructed. She "understood." They stayed in homes, and often traveled through the night. She met black folks and white folks.

At a tavern in Nova Scotia Mary Jane was approached by the tavern keeper's wife. "Annie is about three, her Momma passed 'an she may have kin in Boston. That's all her Pappy was able to tell us. He's gone to sea. It's best she doesn't stay here in the Tavern with no person to look after her. We match folks up as best we can. Will you be able to take her, Miss Washington?"

Annie and James were already playing peek-a-boo. They looked like siblings. Mary Jane thought of her little George and hoped some kind person would escort him to Boston. She prayed silently as she assured the woman she'd be more than pleased to take the child with her and escort her to Boston.[5]

When they finally arrived in Boston, Old George met them and was not the least concerned about having another mouth to feed. He looked for more work and met a man on Atlantic Avenue.[6] George wrote to the Flemings to let them know of his family's safe arrival:

---

[5]Town of Barnstable. *The Seven Villages of Barnstable*, (Town of Barnstable, Massachusetts, 1976).
[6]Caroline Washington Pocknett, written account of newspaper interview of George Washington, c.1910.

Mary Jane found her way here. She and the baby were tuckered out and looking a bit worn for wear. They will regain their strength, and our spirits soar. The news has gone from bad to worse for colored folks. I am mighty obliged for your decision to free my family.
Yours in good faith,
George Washington

George shortly found work down on Cape Cod. Mary Jane was reluctant to leave Boston so soon, but George convinced her of the benefits of moving. There would be people on the Cape willing to help with the children. Since Annie's parents were nowhere to be found, they decided to take her with them on the move; she was a kind child and would help Mary Jane when the new baby arrived.

George planned to save enough money from his farm job to buy land of his own. He worked on a tobacco farm, but found the Cape Cod soil poor for such a crop. While he farmed for others, George looked for a place to buy. Sarah was born on September 12, 1859, and Mary Jane found a community of helpful folks: black, white, Native American, and immigrants including Finns, Jews, Greeks, and Portuguese. They were planning to return to Boston after the growing season. The Cape seemed like a safe, friendly place to be, yet everywhere else slavers were wreaking havoc on black folks. The Quaker Society and Abolitionists were taking the law into their own hands.

Birds' Eye View of - SEASIDE PARK, - Hyannisport, Cape Cod, Mass.

Hyannisport—Happy Hollow was in early Hyannisport, once a large farming area near the sea.

Chapter Seven

Bad News

It was October. They'd been packing their belongings for the move back to Boston, when George came rushing into the room. From the slam of the door and the steely look in his eyes, Mary Jane knew it was more bad news.

"Mary Jane! Captain Brown, him and thirteen other white men and five colored men, they've taken over Harper's Ferry. Your father's been called to put down the insurrection. Dear Lord, what will happen next? Lord, Lord a'mighty, this will topple the mountain. Captain Brown has held off the militia for over thirty hours!" He sat down firmly on a box, slowing his speech and looking off into space. "When Colored men began organizin' and rebellin' in the thirties, we got the Nation's attention. Not just Negro freedom fighters, and conductors, but white men 'an women, Quakers, and churchmen and judges. That made the forties more dangerous. Then the law turned on us in the fifties.[1] Mary Jane, this means war!"

Mary Jane sat immobile, holding little Sarah in her arms. James and Annie sought comfort at her knees, leaning close, frightened at the sound of their father's loud voice.

"I tell you Mary Jane, this is the last straw. If only more of us could be there. Oh Lord be merciful!" He was pounding his fist into his palm, thundering his boots

---

[1] *Barnstable Patriot*, December 6, 1859, sec. none, page 2

on the floor.

The news and the anguish in his face brought tears to Mary Jane's eyes. With sincerity and a stern voice she declared, "Thank heaven you're not there. The militia will slaughter them! They'll all die for nothing!" She was sobbing. "Father could be killed! He's been called for so many dangerous expeditions; in Ohio, and Michigan, war in Mexico, Texas. He's supposed to be on leave, tending to family affairs!"[2]

George calmed down, moved his box close, reaching for Mary Jane, hoping to soothe the upset they both felt.

The Washingtons moved back to Boston over the winter. George could always find work in Boston right on the docks or doing other odd jobs in Suffolk County. They shared quarters with James and Sarah Burton. Mr. Burton was a cobbler and the couple had no children.

Blacksmiths, cobblers, waiters and day laborers found work in the neighborhoods where they lived. It was George's habit to buy milk or bread after his work and he always managed to buy the daily newspaper. George held the *Barnstable Patriot Newspaper* at arm's length as he entered the kitchen. He shook it towards Mary Jane as she continued preparing their noon meal. Unable to wait for her full attention, he began to read.[3]

"New York, Dec. 1.—According to Governor Wise's orders, no one will hereby be permitted to see the prisoners except authorities and clergymen. Brown's interview with the Rev. Mr. Waugh resulted in a difference of

---

[2]Kimberly J. Largent, "The Life of Mary Custas Lee,": eHistory Archive, May 14, 2003,
http://ehistory.osu.edu/world/articles/ArticleView.cfm?AID=67
[3]*Barnstable Patriot,* December 6, 1859, sec. none, page 2

opinion on the question of slavery. He now refuses to see him or any of the Charlestown ministers again."

Mary Jane turned from the stove and gave her complete attention to George. Once he noted her interest, he sat heavily in the chair and continued reading aloud.

"Brown will be executed just before noon on Friday. The Sheriff will take him in charge at 10 o'clock. The last privilege granted to Brown will be the choice between walking and riding to the scaffold. No strangers are admitted here. A guard attends the arrival and departures of every train. Even residents cannot go about after sundown. Mr. Edgerton, member of Congress from Ohio, came here Monday afternoon with a petition from Brown's son for the dead body of his father. This was peremptorily refused, and two hours later Mr. Edgerton went out of town in an open wagon, guarded by four Black Horse Rangers."

Mary Jane sighed deeply and sat beside George. He read silently for a moment and hurrying ahead in the article spoke aloud. "It says further, Baltimore, Dec. 1.— Three passengers by the Western of Baltimore and Ohio railroad were taken out of the cars today on their arrival to Harper's Ferry, by the military and imprisoned. The parties arrested are merchants of Cincinnati, who were on their way to this city. At Grafton they were heard to express themselves quite freely in relation to John Brown and his family, expressing great sympathy for him and them. The conversation was heard by a man, alleged to be a spy of Governor Wise, who telegraphed the account of the matter and a description of the parties. When the cars reached there, the volunteers entered with loaded muskets and carried the men away, not withstanding they earnestly protested their innocence."

George commented, "It seems after these fellow's demise, the Railroad Company refused to sell any tickets to Charlestown till after the execution." George kept reading silently until Mary Jane became impatient and asked, "Does it say anything about Mrs. Brown? How awful, them refusing to give the man's body to his son!"

George responded by reading aloud, "General Talinferro was also present, and Captain Brown urged that his wife be allowed to remain with him all night. To this, the general refused assent, allowing them but four hours. They stood embraced and she sobbing for nearly five minutes, and he was apparently unable to speak. The prisoner only gave way for a moment, and was soon calm and collected, and remained firm throughout the interview. At close they shook hands, but did not embrace, and as they parted, he said—'God bless you and the children'—Mrs. Brown replied—'God have mercy on you,' and continued calm until she left the room, when she remained in tears a few moments and then prepared to depart.

"The interview took place in the parlor of Captain Avis, and the prisoner was free from manacles of any kind. They sat side by side on a sofa, and after discussing family matters proceeded to business."[4]

George noticed tears begin to fall on Mary Jane's cheeks. He stopped reading. "Dear wife, this matter is too somber. I shall put this aside. Let me give you a hand with the stew pot. The children will be fretting soon. We'd best say a prayer for the Browns and be thankful we have our meal."

---

[4]*Barnstable Patriot,* December 6, 1859, sec. none, page 2

John Brown was hung that December of 1859. President James Buchanan's term ended in 1861 and Abraham Lincoln became the sixteenth president. During his two terms the entire nation struggled with bad news. The war divided family loyalties and caused monstrous casualties, both north and south, bringing sad news to many families. Even at the war's end and Lee's surrender, the unthinkable happened. President Lincoln was shot and killed.

***

Groton Leather Board Co.'s Mill, West Groton, Mass.

Groton Leather Board Company Mill, West Groton, Mass.
George Washington and his older sons
worked in this mill.

In 1860, George bought a farm in Royalston, Massachusetts. It was too far from his other work so they moved to Readville, then back to Charlestown. He continued farming and found crops that would thrive in New England soil. When he bought the farm in Shirley, Massachusetts, he also worked in the mill in West Groton. The war began as George predicted. For Mary Jane, bad news continued. Her father's health failed. By 1856, before the war, he himself viewed the institution of slavery as a moral and political evil.[5] Despite this, he fulfilled his duty as a loyal Virginian. General Lee remained true to the Confederacy, a leader of poorly equipped loyal men, and a respected adversary of Union officers.

Mary Jane felt like the life she knew in Maryland died too. A new baby girl, Zilpha, was born in March, the year the war officially began. Joy returned to the family when the Civil War ended in the spring of 1865. That year, their first born son, George, left the plantation. He was thirteen years old when he found his way north. Although he could not read nor write, he made his way safely to Happy Hollow in Hyannis Port, Massachusetts. The reunion was a blessed event and their son shared all the good news he could about the old ones back in Maryland. Young George was of age to enter school, but never did. He, like his parents and siblings, became at home in New England, adopting the speech and traditions of Yankees.

The following year the Washington family made another big decision. They took their five children,

[5]J. William Jones, Personal Reminiscences, Anecdotes, and Letters of Gen. Robert E. Lee (New York: D Appleton and Company, 1875).

George, James, Sarah, Zilpha, and three year old Mary Helen Catherine back south to Queen Anne's, Maryland. That is where they found Old George's sister Henrietta. Tillylish had looked after Skokien and Dahl until they both had passed away. Sophie had a family of her own and made her home in Baltimore. Henrietta was feeble, requiring care which Mary Jane was able to give her. In the spring of 1867 baby Daniel joined the family.

Andrew Jackson had become president. While unpopular with members of congress, he completed his term and was replaced by Ulysses S. Grant. In 1868 negroes became full citizens.

Old George and his sons worked as farm laborers while Mary Jane kept house. Sorrow visited the family when James blew off a wharf at Eastern Shore and drowned. The country was growing and thriving as trains now stretched across the land, but life for the black people remained harsh. After baby Caroline was born, the family again yearned for the peace they had found in Happy Hollow.

Mary Jane bore twelve children, some while they were back south and the last one, when they came back to Massachusetts and moved to Charlestown. That's where baby, Laura, was born in September of 1875.

Chapter Eight

The Freedom of the North

The story that continues is factual. Much of the beginning is also verified. Mary Jane Lee Washington's death record and medical treatment was obtained with legal assistance and is recorded at the Tewksbury Alms House and Asylum. The hospital still functions as a chronic care and rehabilitation facility. Fictional episodes are based on the oral history my grandmother shared about her mother's life along with historical research. *The Freedom in the North* is compiled from the many family letters, massive collections of family photographs, conversations and my personal experiences with my grandmother's siblings.

***

"These winters in Ayer and Pepperell are long and harsh. Mary Jane, I've done my best to make the earth produce. The best soil I've worked was on Cape Cod. I'm still looking to buy a farm there."

"Well, George everyone has made best efforts to make a go of it now we're back in Groton. Even our baby worked out to service. She did a good job at the Academy. She was just about the age of our George, left with the Plantation work, just a small boy."

Laura, working as chambermaid, was not much different from Skokien and Mary Jane in slavery. The family still struggled to make ends meet. It was hard for Laura to give up grade school. At times it seemed the family was working harder than they did when on the plantation.

"I tell you, George, I was never more content than when we lived in Happy Hollow in Hyannis."

George contributed his thoughts. "All the children are grown and making their way in the world. George is a big help. His sons are hard working too. We've seen to it that all the younger children got their schooling, and only Daniel and young Laura haven't gotten married. George and Zilpha's chidren are grown. Mr. Shattuck over at the store says Zilpha's husband is one of his best workers, and our Laura has made good friends here. Susan Shattuck and our Laura have become like sisters! Mary Jane, we've done our best, No one said it was going to be easy."

Mrs. Milo Shattuck, Groton, MA
Store owner's wife and mother to Laura Washington's
good friend, Susan Shattuck.

Nov 9th
Nashua N. H.

My Dear Laura.
I was very glad
to get your nice letter, and
I enclose you 2,00 hoping
it will procure you
some little comfort. I
would gladly do more
for you but being an invalid
my expenses are so much
I cannot do as much for
others as I would like to
do. I was only home three
weeks when I came here
where I expect to stay
through the winter —
I was sorry not to see

Susan Shattuck Letter—page 1.

your sister, but some
one said she was out
of town — I feel very much
for her and sent her a
few things. I also sub-
scribed for the Youth's
Companion for them.

My necessary ex-
penses have been very
large for several years
but my Saviour is
very precious to me
& I know if I am
not perfectly happy it
is because of my lack
of faith in Him

Grant lives as usual in Groton and Albert in Worcester. James has left the store and is in Boston. I had a ride in an Auto a few days since for the first time and liked it— Excuse me for not writing more but my hand is very trembling and I can hardly write at all. I know you will bring your little ones up to love the Sabbath and let me hear from you again soon. Yours with love. Susan P. Shattuck

Susan Shattuck Letter—page 3.

Laura

To Mr. Elias E. Rickards
13 Dartmouth Place
Boston, Massachusetts

June 11, 1893

Dear Elias,
There is so much to do in such a large family. There are eleven of us here you know.
Father still works in the leather mill when the crops are in. He is so pleased this year.
He developed a yellow turnip that has attracted quite a bit of attention.
Brother George is married and he and his wife, Josephine, and their children are with us. There's no room to take in boarders like the railroad men that lived with us at the house in Shirley.
Sarah just moved to Boston when she and Mr. Moffett married.
There is sister Helen and her husband, Bert Munroe. He is working for the Shattuck's at the Store. Brother Dan is living with us. He is still a bachelor and helps Father, and Caroline and her husband are with us. Caroline will soon be returning to Hyannis with her husband, Ben Pocknett.
Sister Zilpha and her husband and children are here too. She married the other Munroe brother. They are all anxious to meet you.

Your beloved friend,
Laura

Laura, the youngest of the Washington children, was being actively courted by a young man from Boston. She would be the last child to marry. Daniel remained a bachelor.

Wedding Plans

"Laura, why must you always fuss so with everything: printed invitations, reception, church ceremony! You forget your mama and papa been slaves? Being free doesn't mean you're privileged!"

Laura continues addressing the dainty envelopes, dipping her quill pen into the narrow-necked, flat little bottle of India ink. Her eyes never meet her mother's. Only the set of her jaw alters the mask of concentration on her face. She finishes writing, and then makes a small, neat stack on the corner of her father's desk.

"Father has gone to get postal stamps, and Elias will be here this evening to help with the planning. Mother, please don't fret!" Laura's plea is amicable. Smiling sweetly at her frowning mother, the eighteen year old girl touches her mother's graying red hair and swishes out of the room. Her mother, Mary Jane sinks helplessly into a high-backed, deep red, velvet chair. Her face still pained, she reaches over to the cluttered roll top desk and picks up an invitation.

"My, my, what beautiful script: she managed to learn a great deal in those few years at school. If this Guinea man hadn't turned her head, she could have done more schooling and be a teacher!" Mary Jane sat up tall in her chair. "My little girl can read and write, just like her

poppa, and has a silver tongue." The beautiful penman-
ship gives no information to Mary Jane. Reading and
writing were skills she and her oldest son, George, never
acquired.

"Mother?" Laura bustles into the room and sees
dejection on her mother's face. "Mother, please don't
worry yourself about the wedding. I can do this. You've
taught me grace and patience. You will have naught to
do except be your gracious self. You have no need to
remind me you were once a slave. I say you were a gifted servant with the best teachers. You have natural wisdom like Solomon, with the patience of Job. Tell me
again about my great grandmother. Now she was a slave,
but only in the minds of her masters!" Both women
smile, as Laura manages to distract her worried mother.
Laura always gets her way.

"Child, you know I barely knew my grandmother!"
Mary Jane's indignant tone jumps from her stern mouth,
but a twinkle pops into her placid eyes. She is proud of
her grandmother, the legendary "runner" from the
Buchanan plantation. Mary Jane gazes at her youngest
daughter, born in freedom just ten years after the end of
the dreadful war.

"Come now, Mother," teases Laura. "You may say I
favor her, but I can't fathom how. I've only known sweet
liberty. I must have some of her impatience. I simply
cannot stand dullards! And I don't fear of anything. The
Almighty gave me none of your demeanor. Sometimes I
feel like I'm from the Milky Way, a way off someplace like
great grandmother found in the swamps; where brain
always defeats brawn, an untouchable place, a fortress
for freedom fighters!"

"Calm yourself, Laura. I declare, my grandmother's

spirit haunts your soul. That brashness will cause your death." She worries to herself that Elias doesn't know this girl's spirit. Her Laura has no idea how a bridle feels.

"When is Elias coming? There's no time for story telling. When your father gets back, he'll be needing rest. He's putting out to sea tomorrow, so he can be back before the wedding. No more shenanigans. Let's set the table, dinner's near ready. Mind your manners tonight", her mother admonishes, "The Lord loveth a kind and gentle spirit."

"You sweet sage, we can do both—set table and talk as well! Is it true that your grandfather was a swamp Indian? Tell again how great grandmother would come right to the plantations and lead people away to the Moses woman."

Mary Jane and Laura tend the food and spread a table fit for the grandest manor house. All the while, Mary Jane re-tells her grandmother's story about the "savage" who spoke in a strange lilting tongue, defied her masters, out-smarted trained bloodhounds, came to the shanty window to steal a glimpse of her precious daughter, Skokien, tending her redheaded baby.

Laura's sisters and brothers, friends and other relatives were pleased when the invitations arrived. Every one in Laura's growing and extended family had come to know and admire Elias. They joked with each other and made Elias feel quite at home. Nephew Albert, her sister Helen's son wrote:

94

S Pepperell Feb 17th 1893

Friend Elias

I thought I would
write you a few lines
we are all quite well now
and hope you are the same
will you please be so kind
as to go and get me some
dandelion greens or spinage
and bring up withe you
for me ~~when~~ to Helen
when you come and bbridge
Albert Munroe and when
you are married we will
come and play to your weddln

and will you please go ~~and~~
out to Watertown and get
Carries fotograph album
and bring with you when
you come it is at Scotts
Helen sends her love to
your mother & Elfrida says
she bringe you her love also
I will be glad to see your
smileing face again as
I will look for you Tuesday
and I wish you would
do one more deed for me
before you come and that
is to drop John Scott for
me. from Albert Munroe.

Albert Munroe Letter

Young Laura
Laura Frances Washington, July 29, 1899.

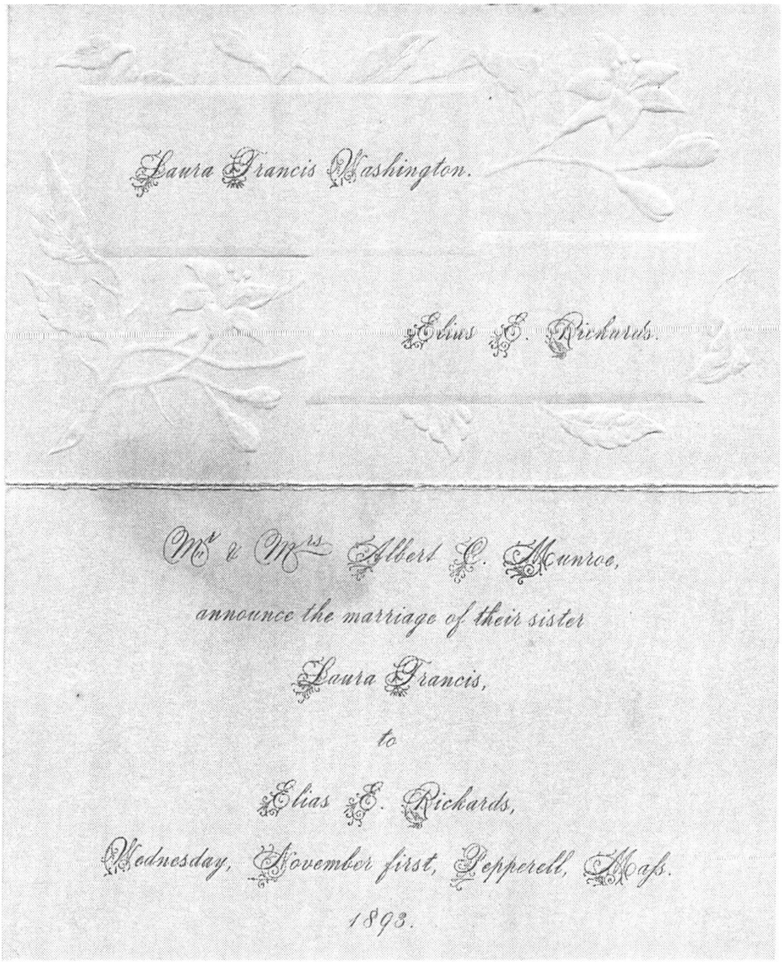

Laura Frances Washington,

Elias E. Richards.

Mr. & Mrs. Albert C. Munroe,

announce the marriage of their sister

Laura Francis,

to

Elias E. Richards,

Wednesday, November first, Pepperell, Mass.

1893.

Laura Frances Washington's wedding invitation—#1.

Laura Frances Washington's wedding invitation—#2.

The Wedding

Elias and Laura were pleased there was no snow on the ground on their wedding day, November 1, 1893. Daniel the best man, and Minnie Holmes, maid of honor, were jubilant.

Laura and Elias were at the church when Elias became anxious and began rehearsing the events leading to this special day. "Your brother Dan will have an easy trip from your Aunt's Mal's in Watertown and Minnie Holms is at your sister Sarah's, right here in Boston. When did you last speak to Reverend Roberts?"

"I wrote him from Pepperell this summer, and I met with him when we came back to Boston. Twelve 0'clock will be here before we know it. Everything is fine. Calm yourself Elias. You hurried over from just across town at Dartmouth Place to worry me with questions?" She smiled and calmed herself.

"I'm saddened that your father passed this year. He and my Father had just gotten to know each other."

"I know both of our fathers were pleased with our wedding plans, but I can't tell if your mother is convinced I can look after you as she expects. Even when I told her of our home in Malden, she looked at me as if we were going off to Canada!"

Laura managed to brighten and smile. She knew her mother was loath to see her last daughter venture off into matrimony.

"This time last year I was living on Cottage Place in Newton. Mother seemed lonesome and longed to be in Happy Hollow down the Cape. I'm sure we will all get there one day soon. Mother loves the Hollow."

"I'm worried about your mother. She seems truly grieved by the loss of her children. It will be good when your parents get to stay on the Cape. Now that your brother has bought the Carney farm in West Hyannis Port, your family won't be moving every season, doing factory work in bad weather and farming when the seasons change. I think that has been harder on your mother than on your father. He is such a hard worker: if it's not farming and factory work, it's off to sea. I've never seen a man so versatile and so willing to do what ever it takes to care for his family. It's no wonder your mother has qualms about me. I'm no farmer, but I certainly know all there is to know about husbandry and horticulture. I make a fair living using my skills."

"When you do gardening for other folks, you're forever teaching them all you know. You should be a professor. What you know about breeding animals is truly a science. Have you ever thought about being a teacher? That was once one of my dreams." A gust of wind and the bang of the big front door interrupted them. "Oh, oh, Elias, I see folks coming into the church!"

The Charles Street AME church filled with well-wishers and family members. The ceremony and the festivities were all that Laura hoped they would be. Family and friends joked with other and danced the evening away. Nephew Albert and his ensemble played the music and Elias surprised every one when he joined them, playing his shiny, new blue enamel accordion.

Mr. and Mrs. Elias Edward Francis Rickards began their life together on 9 Seuntard Place in Malden, Massachusetts.

***

100

"Laura how quickly time moves. Why it only seems like yesterday that we celebrated our wedding. Your family took me in like a birth-son and they keep in touch with us. I enjoy getting mail from Daniel, and your nephews are so close in age they treat you like a sister. My family is not nearly as large as yours, and I know they have no idea what pleasure a close family can bring."

"Elias, your family is just fine. Your mother was overjoyed when I wrote her about our blessed event! Your sister Beatrice sends her best regards. She hopes to visit when the baby is born. Your brother Daniel does his best to keep in touch, even as he travels looking for work. We have another post card from him."

The Washingtons grew up close. That's the only way Mary Jane Lee would have it. She had seen so much separation and loss in her youth. Growing up in the South left its mark on her. The Rickards extended family did not often come to Malden, yet the young couple visited with them in Boston. A branch of Elias' family lived in Philadelphia. They also came to Boston for family events.

***

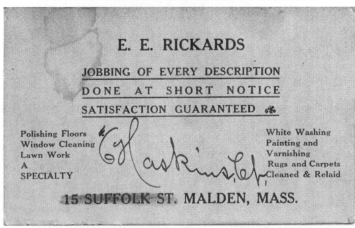

Elias Edward Francis Rickards

Green

Near Revere House.

140 COURT ST.,
BOSTON.

Daniel Rickards
Brother of Elias.

Elfrida Carter Horne
Daughter of Elias' sister Grace Rickards Carter.

Manuel Horne
Elfrida's son.

Grace Bell
Elias Rickards' cousin

Births & Deaths

Baby Ethel Evelyn Rickards was born October 11 of 1894. Grandmother, Mary Jane Lee Washington had been a grandmother many times by now. With twelve years between Laura and her sister Helen, Laura had been an aunt many times. Caroline was closest to Laura in age, with only six years between them. Mary Jane's oldest child, George, worked with his father in Pepperell and Ayer and Shirley. He married Josephine Newcomb on August 13, 1876 and they named their firstborn, Mary Theresa. The next grandchild was a son, William D. Grandmother Mary Jane's next oldest living child, Zilpha Ann, married Joseph Munroe. They named the first two boys Charles Emery and Walter Preston. Mary Jane's daughter Helen (Mary Helen Catherine) married Joe Munroe's brother, Albert Curtis (Bert) Munroe. They already had three boys, William Henry, Albert Danie, and Sherman Emery. Laura's first baby, Ethel Evelyn, had a host of cousins and her mother Laura invited everyone to attend the christening.

Grandmother Mary Jane Lee was unable to make the trip from Happy Hollow. Laura wondered if her father read her letters and then they both forgot. Laura concluded that there was so much happening in the Hollow folks just were not able to come. She explained to Elias, who also wondered at the absence of his in laws. "The first grandchild, Ernest is about fourteen. Looking after a big family is difficult enough and when an adult child dies, the sadness is terribly felt. It is the most awful loss. Recently, George's son, George Lincoln, drowned. There was so much unknown about the circumstances. I'm sure it causes mother to think of her own little Jimmy, drowning at Eastern Shore in Maryland. It gives me the shivers! George and Josephine are still having babies of their own: a stillborn boy, just this past summer. Perhaps there will be no more babies. Josephine is nearing the change."

By 1895 Mary Jane was greatly relieved to stay at Cape Cod in the Hollow, but others began to notice how she missed having all of her children close by. She often withdrew from social events and chose to work with the horses and pitch in with the harvesting.

"George, why do you harvest the corn so soon? You're pulling up the stalks. You know it's best to hand pick the ears and leave the stalks in the ground 'til spring. That's the time to pull and burn them, then put in a different crop. It keeps the soil replenished and you won't pass on a tainted crop. I couldn't even find the oat seed!"

Her indignation confused her husband.

"Why Mary Jane, you are back-in-time thinking about October and full moon corn husking. Our horses pull the tiller and the reaper. This is a big farm, no more hand picking."

He half smiled as he saw his wife's puzzled look, then assured her. "We won't be having the horses trod out the grain like the oxen did in bible time. One day we will be selling our harvest all over the Cape!"

Mary Jane was still ruffled and muttered, "You and those growing grandsons think we women don't know anything about farming? Moses taught me how to use the two handled sickle, near as tall as myself and I can reap those stalks a clean three inches off the ground!"

"Mary Jane, I can see you're still missing the south and the old ways. It was a real social event when the big plantations brought in gangs of workers, white and black, working from sun down into the next day. I do remember those days, but I prefer these times."

He put his arm around her and led her back to the house. He feared she would find that old sickle and prove her point. She continued to complain. "There's nothing for me to do in this house any more. George's wife Josephine and her girls govern the kitchen. It's all I can do to just set the table."

George could see the sadness in her eyes and wondered what he could do to ease her agitation. "Well, Mary Jane, what do you say we go up to Malden and spend some time with Laura and Elias. They'll surely be chores wanting an extra hand. Our other grand children are most full-grown. It might make both you and Laura happy to spend time together. Laura missed seeing you at the Christening. Your strength has certainly come back. Here you are thinking about working the farm!"

When Laura received her father's letter, letting her know her mother was feeling stronger and wanted to visit, she was delighted. That visit was long and the reunion of mother and daughter remained a treasure for both of them. Mary Jane's sadness lifted when Ethyl Evelyn greeted her at the door. The baby walked before she was a year old and with prompting from her mother, called out, "Grandma, grandma, we're happy to see Grandma!"

It was a delightful, long autumn and there was plenty for the women to do. As the weather changed, Mary Jane's mood altered. As darkness fell, she would begin to ruminate. "Laura, I don't think I'll ever get used to these long, cold winters! I think of the warmth and early spring in Maryland. The people there were always so warm. When you children were small, you had opportunity to feel it too, didn't you? Oh, I forget sometimes. You were born up here, so you probably don't even notice. Why when the men were away, there was always a group of working women. Your Elias is away again this week. He's no farmer. Where did you say he must go?"

"Mother, he will not be gone for a week. He's in Boston today getting his fireman's license."

"He's a fireman now?"

"No, Mother, he repairs and runs furnaces for churches and businesses. That's his winter work. In good weather, he does horticulture and tends people's grounds, large estates. He does all that when he's not breeding and selling show animals: chickens and rabbits. Why, he's as busy as father used to be, moving from one seasonal job to another. Now the family has the big farm, you needn't be moving all the time. Doesn't that please you, Mother?"

Mary Jane never answered her daughter's question. The frown and irritation were answer enough to make Laura busy herself in the kitchen. Grandmother Mary Jane closed her eyes and nodded off in front of the fireplace. When she woke up, it was as if the conversation never ended.

"Well the men and boys don't leave much for us women to do but cook and clean and launder. If we didn't have horses to care for, I think I'd just shrivel up and waste away. Have I taught you to use the horsewhip? I don't mean whipping horses, you know. I used to show off to you children doing all the tricks and skills one can do with lisle whip. I just enjoy keeping my skills up. I was ready to harvest the corn with our two-handled sickle. Your father isn't willing to use any of the old ways. There was a special joy when we all joined Moses in the fields. He wasn't reluctant to teach the women any and all skills needed to tend crops or animals!"

Laura sat now, joining her mother in the living room. The baby napped peacefully in her crib. "Mother, you were just a girl then. You certainly didn't hesitate to teach me how to use the whip, or shoot a gun. We never harmed the animals, just moved them quickly along!" Laura laughed as she recalled her mother's lessons tending and training the animals.

"I'm pleased Elias cares for our chickens and leaves me free to work in the house. He prizes those animals. We have eggs and poultry for the table and he gets a good fee for the special breeds. There's so much work sanitizing and cleaning the hen house and rabbit huts. In winter, it's even more difficult."

The Rickard's cottage on Seuntard place had many visitors that winter, as the other sons and daughters, nieces and nephews welcomed invitations to visit Elias, Laura, baby Ethel Evelyn and Grandmother Mary Jane. When spring won the game of tease past the icy cold, Mary Jane became restless and hankered to be home on the farm.

"It's time for me to get back to the Hollow, children. It has been wonderful being here around your family, but it's time to go home."

Laura often found her mother in her kitchen or in the living room before daybreak, tidying up after company left. She seemed to nap during the day after playing with baby Ethel Evelyn or church going, and then her energy would sneak out when the family was sleeping. Laura missed her all the same, and looked forward to getting her to make another long visit when the next baby came. She knew, but didn't mention her "condition" to her mother.

Gladys Thorndike Rickards was born on January 28 1896. With a two year old and a new baby, there was plenty to keep a young mother busy. Elias found his work often took him away for long hours, both winter and summer. Letters among the siblings usually kept the whole family up with each other's lives. When Laura wrote to her father about the coming event, his return letter mostly referred to the success of the farm.

Dear Daughter Laura.
Things are going well. The maple trees are producing great amounts of sap and the farm is expanding. We harvest products that give us profit clear through the winter. The yellow turnip is still a best seller and stores well. New customers by word of mouth guarantee another good season. The weather has stayed mild so we can harvest carrots from the garden all year. Your Mother finds it hard to rest at night, but she hasn't lost her energy. She wishes you all well, and sends her love. Send photographs.
Your loving father.

Zilpha Washington Munroe
Born March 13, 1861
Married Joseph Munroe
Her Daughter Mamie took in Hessie.

**Bernice Munroe, Zilpha and Joseph Munroe's daughter.
She married Harold from the Cape.**

Freddie Munroe, son of Helen (Mary Helen Catherine)
Washington Munroe.

**Helen Dupee Thibou and cousin Dorothy Dupee Chester,
grandchildren of Zilpha Washington Munroe.**

Ancestor Chart

George Buchanan Washington

Born October 20, 1813 in Howard County, Maryland

Died, October 19, 1911 in Barnstable County, MA

Married: Mary Jane Lee

(date and place to be confirmed)

Mary Jane Lee

Born circa 1833 in Fredrick County, MD

Died, December 30, 1896 in Tewksbury, MA

Children

George Thomas born April 16, 1853
in Fredrick County, MD

James H. born 1857 in Fredrick County, MD

Sarah Jane born September 12, 1859 in MA

Zilpha L. born March 13, 1861 in MA

Mary Helen Catherine born March 4, 1863 in MA

Daniel born May 4, 1867 in MD

Caroline Ellen born August 8, 1869 in MD

Laura Frances born September 21, 1875 in MA

Chapter Nine

The Winter of 1896

Laura wrote to her mother, feeling assured that her father or one of brother George's children would read it to her.

> *My Dear Mother,*
> *Baby Ethel has taken a real shine to her*
> *baby sister Gladys. The baby can hardly*
> *cry, Ethel rushes to rock the cradle and*
> *wants to be second mother. Winter has*
> *been harsh this year. I hope the waterfront*
> *keeps it milder in the Hollow. Diphtheria is*
> *epidemic in Malden. Many of the adults are*
> *suffering too. I've not brought the girls to*
> *church and will surely delay the*
> *Christening. I do hope you are well enough*
> *to come this time.*
> *Your loving daughter, Laura*

Laura knew her brother's oldest son William had left the farm to go out to sea. He did shell fishing, carpentering and worked in a restaurant in Boston. The nieces and nephews wrote about their lives, her sisters and brothers visited and in rough weather, wrote newsy letters. When baby Gladys Thorndike came down with diphtheria, Laura wrote to her sister Caroline who lived in Hyannis.

My dear sister Caroline,
Father rarely answers my letters and I fear
things at the farm are not going well.
Mother was not able to travel when I last
invited her to come to Malden. Father does
not do well expressing difficulties. I trust
you will be able to share this news at the
farm.
This has been a very bad winter and I
have some very sad news. Our baby
Gladys Thorndike died this Sunday at 5:00
pm. She was just seven months and 14
days old. There is more sadness. Ethyl
Evelyn tumbled down the stairs in a deliri-
um of fever. She is inconsolable with the
loss of her sister. She asks for her and we
must hold her day and night. Elias keeps
watch at night so I can manage the day. I
don't know how Mother will bear the news.
Each time the family suffers a death
Mother goes into deep sadness and silence.
I've written Daniel and the others. It's not a
good time to visit and there is nothing one
can do for us at this time. The diphtheria
and whooping cough are claiming adult
lives too. Do keep well and give my love to
all.
Your mourning sister, Laura

Mary Jane did not hear the news at all. She wasn't at the farm and had not been there since June 15 of that year.

***

The two Georges were saddened by Laura's news, and deeply worried about how Laura would handle the failed attempts they had already made in trying to care for mother, Mary Jane.

"Father, I'm not certain what to do about mother. Josephine has done her best to keep her from clattering in the kitchen during the night, and now she's taken to wandering off when she gets upset."

"Son, I don't know what to think. Sometimes she's clear as a bell and the next moment she's fussing with me about some chore not getting done just right. She naps during the day and I never feel her slipping out of the room at night."

Young George continued weighing his circumstances, "Our baby is due next month and I fear it's too much on Josephine. It seems Mother took the wash out to the shed and started putting laundry into the maple sap! She gets right contrary and it's all I can do to calm them both down!"

Father continued with the quandary. "With Will and his wife in Boston and the girls all married with family, it's not right to put it all on Laura. She has her own family to look after. Your mother did well there. Maybe Dan can look after her. He and Aunt Mal can keep her busy. Son, that seems to be at the bottom of all this. Mother just wants something useful to do!"

Urgent conversations had been exchanged as Mother Mary Jane's condition worsened.

Young George reviewed all that had been done to resolve the problem of Mary Jane Lee's decline, "Father, I sent for Caroline once or twice when I found Mother was having a rough day, but Carrie's laundering business is mighty heavy these days. She kept Mother there for a time. That's probably what sparked the confusion with the maple sap. We best call on Carrie and see what we can figure out."

When the two Georges consulted with Carrie, she had more concerns. "Mother over-works herself in the barn. Then she just sets outside, looking as if she's not sure of her whereabouts. I just keep an eye on her, but it does worry me. I thought maybe she's uncomfortable being away from the farm. She doesn't fuss with me like I noticed she does with Josephine. Some thing has to be done. We don't want her harming herself. You say she wanders during the night? That's not a good sign. Do you think we should consult a doctor?"

Father decided, "Perhaps we should. I've also written brother Daniel, to see if he and Mal can look after her for a spell."

Dan and Mal lived in Watertown on the outskirts of Boston. They followed their plan and when Dan was unable to keep his mother from leaving the house to go back to the Hollow at any hour of day and night, they took the doctors advice and placed her in care. It was not without much thinking and consulting that the men came to the sorrowful decision.

The first visit son George, Father and Josephine made to Tewksbury went fairly well, but in July, Mary Jane noticed Josephine's trim figure.

"Well, now" She asked. "Did you finally birth that big baby?"

Mary Jane was clearly pleased to see them all and her mind was sharp. She also thought it meant she would be going home soon, especially when they saw how well she was doing.

Josephine looked to the men for a cue. They were mute, so she just said it as gently as she could without letting her own grief color the words. "Mother, I am fine now. The baby was a boy. He was born still, never took a breath."

Mary Jane heard and understood, then went silent. The small talk that followed left them all somber. When they left, Mary Jane feared she would never see the Hollow again. She became quiet and went silent. The whole family fell silent.

***

Three months passed before Old George wrote to his youngest daughter.

> *My dearest Laura,*
> *I am at a loss to tell you how sorry I am to hear that you lost Ethyl Evelyn Saturday night, at just past her second birthday. I know you have heard by now that we had to place your mother in the care of the state. That's what the doctor recommended. We could not bring ourselves to talk much about this. Mother was doing well at first and we thought we might get her back here on the farm, but when Josephine lost her boy, Mother took it very hard. That is why we have not carried any more sad news to her. When you are feeling up to it, please go and visit with her. She does ask for you and most times, she is quite her-*

self. My heart is grievously heavy for the
lot of us. This has been a most troublesome
year.
With my fondest wishes for your recovery,
I remain, your loving Father.

Laura had already buried her two daughters before she was able to go to Tewksbury.

Chapter Ten

Healing Time in the Hollow

Grief hung like ocean mist muting the entire family. Each death made a sad revisiting. The rifts and accusations, the regrets and self-doubts, the blame, and the self-blame visited each one. It was Elias who came up with a plan. His sweet name for Laura was Babe.

"Babe, why don't we move to the Cape? Your family has tried so hard to regain the closeness we all had when Mother Washington was alive. Even folks in Groton have kept close contact with the family. I see you received another letter from Susan Shattuck. The postmark tells me she's back home working in the store. All your nieces and nephews have done well by us, visiting and writing. It's we adults who have had the hard time. I've seen how silence has wounded your father and brothers."

Laura appeared solemn as the thought of returning to Happy Hollow provoked a stream of memories.

Elias continued, "Many of the estates I'm tending are down that way. The owners go to Maine and Vermont for the summer to avoid the summer beach folks!" He laughed at the irony of such decisions, then took Laura in his arms and whispered. "This house holds some sadness for us too. I've seen some pretty nice places we can rent."

Before the turn of the century, the Rickards family moved from Malden to West Hyannis Port. Siblings came from Hyannis, Pepperell, Lawrence and Leominster to visit on the Farm. Old George's door was never locked and the family regrouped, especially in summer! The Rickards family hosted friends and relatives and often visited Boston.

It was 1900; Laura was a vibrant woman of twenty-four years and Elias a dapper young man of thirty-two. Salty air, sea breezes and sunshine heightened their happiness, along with the wonders of a new baby on the way. All of the Washingtons began to prosper. They had multiple businesses serving all of Cape Cod: the truck farm, carpentry, trash removal, clamming and fish mongering.

No one was prepared for the oldest grandchild to bring another sorrow to the family. Marriage for colored girls was challenging. Colored men labored very hard and had to travel to earn a living wage. It was not uncommon for colored 'cousins' to marry: not to amass or retain wealth and power as the Europeans, but due to the need for small communities of color to cluster together. Every family member had to work to make ends meet. The clusters were often geographically separated and colored folks travelled to nearby communities to socialize with extended family members and friends.

Working class whites, Indians and immigrants created unions with colored folks in places like Cape Cod. They worked together and lived compatibly. Mary Jane and Old George's daughter Caroline married a Native American, Ben Pocknett. George and Mary Jane's oldest son married Josephine Curtis, daughter of Teresa Cahoon (Granny) from Spain. The older daughters married while the family still worked and lived in Groton, Ayer and Pepperell. They raised their families there and in Lawrence and Leominster. Sarah and Helen moved on to Boston. Dan, unmarried, lived in the same areas as his older sisters. Young George and his offspring made Cape Cod their home and young Laura and Elias also lived on or near the Cape until their children were school aged.

Mary Theresa Washington, Old George and Mary Jane's oldest grandchild, was the first of the next generation to marry. She was nick named Mamie, and she married a colored man, Joe Hill. He was not a close cousin, nor an Indian, just an ordinary struggling colored man of humble beginnings, and he sure did prize his new bride! The *Barnstable Patriot Newspaper* chronicled their union.

Mamie married in 1895, the year before grandmother Mary Jane Lee Washington's admission to the Tewksbury Alms House and Asylum. Young George's daughter was a bride of eighteen years. Old George had some misgivings about this young man.

"George, that lad has never known 'family'—tossed away at a young age as he was."

"Well, Pa, he has found steady work and the two of them are so smitten with each other, it seems wise to sanction a marriage. Mamie is a 'good' girl and Joe certainly adores her. It's true, his family has seen some hard times and Joe suffered some because of it, but what colored man hasn't had hardship of one kind or another. We all have to make the best of what the Lord provides. They are of age and I'll give them a helping hand if need be."

"Well son, I suppose that's all anyone can do. It will be interesting to see if his family comes to the fore. It's not likely: since we come to know Hill was born and brought up in Provincetown at the alms house and was a town ward in his younger days. It seems his mother

126

married Ebenezer Cahoon of Happy Hollow. The woman was of Spanish offspring: her mother having been brought to Hyannis by a sea captain in whose family she was a domestic. They seem to continue struggling through hard times."

The wedding went as planned and the young couple lived in West Yarmouth not far from the elder Washington's permanent home. Caroline counseled her niece, assuring the young bride that she could always have the support of her family. Mamie complained, "Joe is so jealous without cause! Aunt Carrie, what makes a loving husband so confused? I've given him no cause to treat me so."

"Treat you how, child?"

"Well, he demands to know where I am every minute! Even if we go to the Farm together to help out, he queries all the men needing to know if they are relatives or hires, as if I'm unsafe around my own family!"

Caroline again reminded her young niece that she could always confide in her family and if need be, "Let Joe know that such behavior could ruin a good marriage. There must be trust in all good relationships."

Mamie did keep close to her father and older relatives. Laura and Elias had attended the wedding and were a bit dismayed when Carrie noted in her letter that the young couple was having difficulties. Laura assured Elias, "If Mamie doesn't assert herself she'll be a miserable woman. Sister Carrie believes the two will separate, just to give Joe the message, that kind of 'love,' that possessive kind, ruins a friendship and can destroy a marriage."

They did separate, twice. Young George supported his now 22 year old daughter, assuring her that if the marriage couldn't survive, she could always return to the Farm, and that's just where she was when Joe sought her out. They had exchanged strong words at their home in West Yarmouth, and Mamie made it clear, "Raising children in a home fraught with arguing and threats of harm just will not happen!"

It was Friday evening. Mamie and her two sisters, Flora age ten and Josephine (Pinky) age 14, were walking from the Farm into the Port village. They heard Joe call out.

"Mamie!"

As she turned towards him, he shot her! The sisters were frozen with terror. Folks nearby at the Kerr cottage ran out when they heard the gun shots and the shrieking cries of the girls.

"Stay away! Stay back." Joe shouted at them as he waived the smoking Remington army revolver. They knew Joe, recognized him at once. They did not stand back, so he ran off. Mamie was dead. The close range shot entered her mouth causing instant death.

The authorities were notified by telegram. Officer Letteney and Deputy Sheriffs Allyn and Bradford went in pursuit. The district police officer, Letteney arrested Joe Hill as he ran off towards the swamp in West Yarmouth. Although he pleaded "not guilty," the witnesses and the investigating officers' testimony influenced the judge to declare the crime premeditated and heinous. The trial was re-set.

Her sisters informed the authorities, "Mamie fell to the ground, Joe came close, we couldn't move for fear and he put the gun to her face and shot her again!!"[1]

---

[1] "Hill Kills His Wife," *Yarmouth Register* (June 24, 1899).

Mary Jane Lee Washington was spared the horror of this tragedy. Mamie perished at the hands of a person who was most certainly insane. Young Joe Hill was deemed insanely jealous and was remanded to prison. When Joe made a bid to be released, Mamie's brother William made sure the bid was denied.

"Let him rot in jail!" Folks on the Cape commented, "The poor bugger went blind, never left the jail."[2]

The author also spent many summers on Cape Cod and always visited the farm in Hyannisport. There was something creepy about walking toward Pinkie's cottage. The path lead out of sight of the farmhouse and as a young person, I never dared to walk that path. There was a story about someone getting killed in that field. Researching old Cape Cod newspapers explained what happened and illustrates how long fear and sadness remain in a family.

---

[2]This crime repeats in the next two generations. Vera Drummond Patrice (cousin) and Claudia Joy Cato Pearsall (godchild, niece) were both murdered by jealous husbands.

Family Group

George Thomas Washington

Born 1853 in Fredrick County, MD

died 21 January 1958 Barnstable County, MA

Married Josephine D. Newcomb 31 August 1876

Josephine Newcomb

Born 26 May 1859 in Barnstable County, MA

died 1941 in Barnstable County, MA

Young George Thomas' and Josephine's Children.

Mary Theresa (Mamie): born 1877, died 23 June 1899

William D.: born 23 December 1879, died 1980

Josephine V.: born 27 April 1885

Florence (Flora): born 26 September 1887

died 19 October 1987

George L.: born 1 April 1890

Hanson (Hanney): born 23 August 1892

died 5 September 1973

Wesley (Wessey): born 20 May 1894

Sarah Jane: born February 1898

Frederick Lawrence: born 29 August 1901

died 1 November 1970

Life Goes On

At 5:00 o'clock on Sunday evening July 22, 1900, Elsie Viola Rickards was born in Hyannis, Massachusetts. Laura found herself surrounded by family and friends, and Elias kept busier than ever. The new century was bustling with inventions and conventions. He showed his prize breeds at County Fairs and won ribbons. He worked as janitor and fireman in the town hall, and continued the seasonal work of horticulture. The young couple soon found themselves moving seasonally to accommodate the variety of work available. Laura's next pregnancy was complicated. She developed gestational diabetes and had worrisome symptoms. Their doctor advised them to go to Woman's Lying In Hospital as precaution.

It was seven in the evening on Saturday, October 17, 1903 when the nurse ushered Elias into the room. He kissed and hugged his sweet Babe and placed his finger in his baby Dorothy Lee's hand. She pulled his finger right to her mouth.

"Oh darling, I know what you want, but you won't get it from this scrubbed hand!"

The room burst with laughter as the nurse positioned Laura to nurse the baby.

"Oh, Elias, I feel sooo much better. They just might let me go home before this week ends. I know Elsie Viola is not wearing you out. She has grown so quickly and can really help out around the house. She mimics everything I do, so I just give her the dust rag and let her join me! You simply can not stay away from your work for another week."

"We are doing just fine, Laura. You shall stay here as long as the doctor thinks necessary. Nurse how is her sugar? They were very concerned those last weeks. That's why we came here to Boston. The hospital in Hyannis thought they might have to take the baby by surgery if the sugar and swelling increased."

"Well Mr. Rickards, you'll have to consult the doctor about that, but I can tell you most women who have the toxicity, get right back to normal once the baby is born."

The nurse's smile put them at ease. Laura did not stay a full two weeks in the hospital like most mothers of that time.

Migration

When baby Dorothy was four, the family moved to 131 Ellsworth Street in Brockton. It was near many of Elias' contacts in Malden and not a long ride to Hyannis. Trolley cars and trains allowed the family to gather more frequently.

"Babe the girls haven't been to the Hollow nor seen their cousins since the move. Now that we're settled in, a trip to Hyannis might be timely, or perhaps we could have the family with us for a week end."

"Oh, I don't know Elias, getting acquainted at church, Elsie so new to her school, having the family here may be more enjoyable than trucking off to the Hollow. There's always so much going on at the Farm. People just dropping in, getting the girls settled for sleep. It's not always easy." Her voice hushed.

"Elias, listen! Dorothy and Elsie are playing with their dolls. It's eerie hearing the names they've given them: Gladys and Ethel. Do you suppose we have done so much mourning at the loss of our babies, these little girls are trying to bring them back to us?"

"Well, Babe, I think it's a good thing to keep memories alive. Why, when you stayed up so late those first days, setting this house straight, I nodded off to sleep, and felt your mother's presence. She was so wont to be up and about in the quiet of the night, straightening up the house. It was a pleasant memory, comforting. You are so like your mother at times: restless until everything is in order. And the first time I heard the girls fussing over their baby dolls, crooning the names, Gladys and Ethel, only the fondest memories of our babies came to mind. That was such a hard year, one we shall never forget."

"They say time heals all wounds, but I swear to you Elias, Mother's passing was the worst, the very worst of times." Laura paused, then turned to stare at the wall behind her. "It gives me solace to have her portrait. I look into her eyes and pray for her deliverance. She was a prayerful woman, not so much a church-goer, but mighty prayerful."

Mary Jane Lee Washington

Laura coaxed the playing children into the bedroom, where they laid out their Sunday clothes and prepared for the routine Saturday night bath.

The family was active in the church. The girls were baptized at the Lincoln Congregational Church on Easter Sunday, April 15, 1906. They attended church school there and began grade school. Elias continued to work multiple jobs in the general area.

Their first Brockton address in 1906 was 356 North Montello Street, where they had a big back yard. From there they went to Hyannis Port until September then back to Brockton, 22 Ridgeway Court.

***

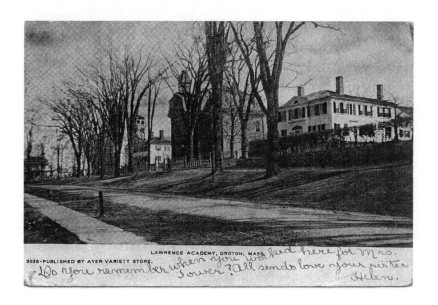

LAWRENCE ACADEMY, GROTON, MASS.
3036-PUBLISHED BY AYER VARIETY STORE.

Do you remember when you worked here for Mrs. Jower? All sends love your sister Helen.

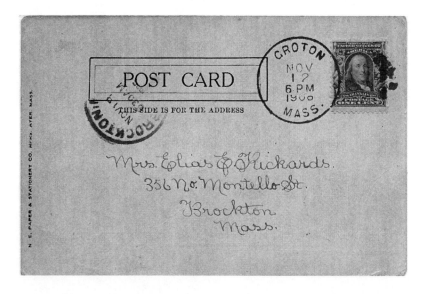

POST CARD

THIS SIDE IS FOR THE ADDRESS

N. E. PAPER & STATIONERY CO. MFRS. AYER, MASS.

CROTON
NOV
12
6 PM
1906
MASS.

Mrs. Elias E. Rickards.
356 No. Montello St.
Brockton
Mass.

**Postcard from sister Helen (Mary Helen Catherine)
Washington Munroe to her sister Laura Frances
Washington Rickards.**

In 1909 the trustees of the church where Elias was employed as janitor, sent regrets terminating his services. This unexpected termination seemed unjustified and puzzled Elias. He found more work in Malden, moved to 6 Haskins Street and remained in Malden until 1912. Their last baby was born while they still lived in Malden. It was late summer, July 30, 1912 when this little one joined the family. She was the pride and joy of the Washington and Rickards families. She was a bright child, benefitting from the attention of her two sisters and all the adults who visited. A "bright skinned" baby tended to be greatly admired by most colored folks. There were advantages, even in slavery days. Mary Jane Lee was a "light skinned" negro and this baby was clearly on the light side of the color spectrum. It made mother Laura worry that the baby got so much attention. "She'll be spoiled rotten if you girls don't stop pampering her!"

Baby Evelyn Louise Rickards Walley
Born July 30 1912.

The Rickards Family

Baby Evelyn Louise was just four months old when the unexpected telegram came.

DECEMBER 2, 1912
9:13 AM WORCESTER, MA TO:
MRS. L. F. RICKARDS
442 EASTERN AVE., MALDEN, MA
"LOCK UP HOUSE LEAVE EVERYTHING
COME TODAY SURE."
E.E. RICKARDS

Laura dropped everything and arrived in Worcester with no idea where the family might live. Letters were forwarded to 27 Carroll Street, Worcester. Dorothy Lee was in the fourth grade at Thomas Street School and the school experience was ugly. They moved to a boarding house at 3 Hudson Place in Worcester. By 1920, letters were again forwarded to 19 Rodney Street. The migrating family sought and found improved social conditions where their growing daughters attended socials, and dances in and about the Beaver Brook area of Worcester. There were many family visits to Cape Cod, Boston and Leominster. The cousins wrote and visited frequently while Laura did laundry and Elias tended and repaired boilers and furnaces. He was janitor at the Union Hill School and continued to work for the City of Worcester until his death. It was 1921 when letters were addressed to 4 Ellen Street in Worcester. Elias rented the nine room cottage at four Ellen Street from Antonio Lucci in July. Many photographs indicate these were happy times. The family took in and cared for state children. Elsie and

Dorothy were courted. Elias made plans to build a home for Laura. Their lease was for three years costing $25.00 per month. It was here that he built his coops and animal shelters.

**Evelyn Louise Rickards (age 7) on the left
with grandchild of Helen Washington Munroe her
cousin Cecile Thomas (age 10) only child of Alfreda
Munroe and Dan Thomas**

**Dorothy Lee Rickards born 10-17-1903 (on left) with
Elsie Viola Rickards born 7-22-1900 (on right).
Taken February 29, 1920.**

Bells of 1916
Elsie Rickards top row far left,
Dorothy Rickards front row far right
With friends: Inez Green, Rebecca Dozer, Molly Cooper,
Susie Green, Alma Hampton, Georgiana Dozer,
and Ella MacDowell

Epilogue

Laura remained stalwart: a daughter who would make her mother proud. She embodied Mary Jane Lee Washington's legacy, being a woman prepared to bear and forebear. As Laura matured, she set her jaw firmly. Her speech was precise and deliberate. Only her eyes kept their girlish twinkle. She could hold a sober face yet smile with her eyes. Elias maintained his dapper posture. His horticulture and animal breeding skills increased. He won medals, took jobs where ever they were available and remained the bread winner of his family. Old George and the Washington men remained close and supportive to their in-law brother.

As Old George summoned Mary Jane Lee to come north, be it Canada or Boston, she followed him to a strange new place, so did her youngest daughter Laura, leave her familiar home in Brockton and the comforts of four Ellen Street.

The last move was to 6 Ellen Street. The elder daughters married. Laura and Elias and their youngest daughter Evelyn Louise moved to 6 Ellen Street in the house Elias built. With this last move their wedding gifts and best china remained unpacked, stored in the attic and back shed, awaiting a time when the small cottage with it's tar paper covering would be made a permanent, multiple room home. That never happened.

Laura & Elias Rickards
On their newly acquired property
at 6 Ellen Street, Worcester, MA.

Mrs. Laura F. Rickards' Model T Ford.

When we last left Laura, she was looking forward to the house Elias planned to build on that large tract of land across the road. She left the comforts of four Ellen Street with its spacious rooms, lovely porch and yard, to live in a temporary one room large cabin, with four windows and two attached sheds. Another free standing shed stood to the left in back and the outhouse was just a short walk behind the cabin, no water, no electricity! This granddaughter was instructed to go to the outhouse to "shake the dew off your lily."

Elias built a large chicken house up on a ridge of an adjoing lot. It had high ceilings and was several feet longer than the cabin. Behind the cabin there was another cluster of coops, cages and animal runs brought over from the rental house. Mary Jane Lee's portrait always brought solace and hope to the aging Laura. Throughout all the years Laura occupied the humble cabin, it was hung proudly on the cabin wall. Once electricity was installed and the new stove arrived, it looked more like home. On that cast iron blue enamel and shiny chrome stove, she brewed sulfur and molasses spring tonics, and made the best oyster stews and fish and corn chowders. Laura was very proud of her decision to buy a model T Ford. Neither she nor Elias ever procured a driver's license. Young Evelyn Louise became the designated driver.

Model T & Evelyn
Evelyn Louise Rickards
Teen Age Driver

Hardship showed on handsome Elias and his stately bride as they reached their mature years. Their bodies and their expressions mirrored their stalwart determination to succeed. The family and close relatives stuck together, savoring the delights and happiness their closeness assured.

Laura Frances Washington Rickards
and husband Elias Edward Frances
in front of their home at 6 Ellen Street, Worcester, MA
circa 1934.

That humble home remained a gathering place for visiting family and friends and when hurricane or fire threatened, Laura demonstrated her attachment to her little home on six Ellen Street. Grandpa Elias died in November 1937 and Grandma Laura was living alone in 1940 when the unexpected happened.

Grandma Laura

From the tiny window her profile was clearly visible. Her neck was rigid and her square shoulders pressed deliberately against the back of an overstuffed platform rocking chair. The upholstery was completely covered by layers of hand crocheted throws, just as the plumpness of her body was layered by a knitted shoulder wrap, apron, long dress and afghan covering her knees.

"Is she deaf?" A fireman asked the neighbor who peered through the window. The closed porch on the south side of the small house had two stout doors, both firmly latched and locked by the stoic Laura who sat inside.

"No, she hears you. She's shaking her head. She's not coming out. She's lame, but she moves well with a cane," reported the neighbor.

Laura's knees no longer flexed well and were supported on a low hassock. She told her grandchildren that her knees had worn out due to the many miles she had trudged through waist high drifts of snow, walking to school and to service up in Ayer and Pepperell. Soft wooly lined slippers, stretched over time, loosely hugged her slightly swollen feet, which were covered by long, thick, tan colored cotton stockings.

"They say her mother got senile and washed her clothes in maple sap. She got to running off and had to

152

be put away," offered a voice from a small group now gathering in the yard.

"Well she must be crazy if she thinks we can save this old tar-papered shack!" The fireman grumbled. "Look, the men can't even contain the brush fire up on the ridge. The chicken house is going up now. We were trying to save some of those back sheds, but it's no use." He beckoned to the other firefighters to abandon their spot on the hill and join him. "We can keep those sparks from touching off the roof. Come on men! Hose over the house! There's an old lady in there that won't come out!"

Steam rose from the water spray over the house: smoky, spark filled air smelled of burning feathers and chicken droppings.

"Jan Rickards had show hens, and pigeons, and rabbits," piped a young voice. "Oh no, they all got burned up, nuthin left now, nuthin!" He ran off to spread the news to the squad of school children who were beginning to break from their usual parade and run toward the fire engines.

"Captain, why in the hell don't we just chop the door or bust that damned window and haul her out of there?"

"Keep these kids away, Joe," barked the captain as he squared his shoulders, steeled his eyes and gave a last authorative try.

"You must come out!" As he shouted he banged the outer door with the butt of his axe. Laura stared straight-ahead, avoiding eye contact. Her firm throaty voice was clearly heard.

"No!"

She began to rock slowly. Her toothless jaw set firmly, making hollows in her cheeks, accenting her mixed heritage. Her bronze skin bore more lines than wrinkles and the grayness of her hair appeared dark because it was smoothed slickly back with Vaseline. It was twisted in an unseen knot at the base of her neck. The sharpness of her eyes was easily noted, as she did not require glasses. Laura rocked more deliberately, rhythmically, in response to the fireman's last plea.

"Gram, Gramma" shrieked one of the school children, who now mingled with the bewildered adults.

"Get that kid! Grab that one." Two crying little girls raced for the porch door.

"Lift that one to the window," snapped the captain. "She'll come out now!"

Without any prompting, the child screamed, "Please, Gram, please, come out!"

Preventing the girls from running to the house, the firemen instructed the neighbors to hold the sobbing girls while all the hoses cascaded gallons of water over the house; the only building left standing at 6 Ellen Street. The steam and smoke dwindled to smoldering lumps of old timbers and the air held the stench of wet ash and burned chicken flesh. The cascade of water saved the house. The outhouse was the only other structure saved. I was one of those screaming, terrified children and did not come to understand Gram's logic until I was an adult. She knew the firefighters were only focused on saving her life. She was focused on saving a home for the generations to come. Through the small window a neighbor spoke to Laura.

"Mrs. Rickards, these children are near worried to death! Are you all right?"

Laura's eyes never blinked. Her voice was not loud, but was clearly heard by the huddled group of neighbors, firemen and granddaughters.

154

"The house goes, I go."

***

The struggle each generation has faced since Mary Jane Lee Washington walked to freedom from involuntary servitude made her progeny strong. No monetary inheritance could have served us as well as the fortitude she bequeathed. Her youngest child, Laura Frances Washington Rickards (my grandmother) repeatedly told me in her oral tradition, and showed me by her determined, tenacious life, how to benefit from my inheritance. I am eternally grateful for these gifts. That determination displayed itself in Fallashaday, the fictionalized African ancestor and the real characters in *The Roan*. I was privileged to know and spend years with my maternal grandmother, Laura Washington, and five of her siblings: George, Dan, Carrie, Sarah and Helen. I am also in possession of Mary Jane Lee Washington's portrait and have spent decades confirming and unearthing facts to corroborate the family legends passed on by Laura, the youngest of Old George and Mary Jane's children. She lived to be eighty-six years old.

Facts
There were many happy times on four Ellen Street. The Rickards girls became women when they lived there. Elsie Viola married Heywood Hampton: a young man of color born in Alexandria, Virginia in 1897. He served in the military, ended up in Worcester where the young couple took up housekeeping and started a family. Proud young Aunt Evelyn is photographed with her new nieces and nephews and a baby whom the family cared for.

Betty Hawkins was a state child; close in age to Evelyn Lorraine, the Hamptons first born. There are many photographs of Evelyn Louise from infancy through her teen years in Worcester. She was the teen-age driver of the Model T Ford, chauffeuring her father all over New England to Fairs and competitions where he won honors, ribbons and prizes. Those days she had a mischievous "I dare you" look in her eye.

Evelyn Louise Rickards Walley circa 1921.

**Dorothy Lee Rickards Perkins Barrow
and friend Robert (Bob) Walker
August 28, 1919.**

Dorothy Lee was the next to marry while they lived at number four. Her husband was William Dempsey Perkins born in Worcester. His folks came to the city from North Carolina. Their first born was also a girl, Lois Marie.

Evelyn was the last to be courted. She married Reginald Walley: a musician, dancer, and former military man. This author's earliest memory of Evelyn was dancing. I was four years old, dancing along with guests at the Walley wedding. She wore a flattering blue dress, the filmy flowing kind that women wore in the nineteen twenties. The Rickards women were masters at crafts. It's likely she sewed the wedding dress herself. That union bore no children. Evelyn remained a devoted aunt.

The Washington sisters and their daughters worked together cooking, brewing homemade root beer, sewing, knitting, crocheting, and making hair brushes from pigs bristle. Laura Washington Rickards embodied her mother's features and attributes: strong jaw, piercing eyes, sculptured cheek bones and straight hair. Red hair continues to re-appear even unto Mary Jane's great grand children—David Lee, son of Elsie Viola, and Audrey Elizabeth, daughter of Dorothy Lee—and the great, great grandchildren—Deborah Celeste, daughter of Lois Marie, Dorothy Lee's first born. The Washington women held their mouths tightly shut until they had something deliberate and meaningful to say, and you had better listen! Never did I see my grandmother "high strung" or anxious. She was unflappable, ready to face whatever fate put in her path.

A New Generation

**Adults: L-R: Evelyn Rickards Walley, Dorothy
Rickards Perkins Barrow (Daughters of Laura F.
Washington Rickards) and Audrey Barrow Brown
(Daughter of Dorothy Barrow)
In Evelyn's Arms, Elizabeth Brown (Daughter of
Audrey), In Dorothy's Arms, (Mary) Mia Carter,
Daughter of Shirley Barrow Carter, In Audrey's
arms, Dorothy Brown, her daughter.
Standing in the foreground, Laura (Carter) Rickards,
Daughter of Shirley Barrow Carter (the photographer).**

There is a sad irony in how aging affected Laura. In her confusion she left her home on six Ellen Street attempting to walk to The Hollow on Cape Cod. She fell on one of these attempts and broke her wrist. The medical team was reluctant to give anesthesia to an elderly diabetic woman who recently had a meal, but the fracture was days old and the healing had gone awry. The physician informed her:

"Mrs. Rickards, your bones have already begun to knit, but if we don't re-break that wrist and set it properly, you will not be able to use this hand. Now, if you can tolerate it I can snap it quickly, and then wrap it in plaster to hold it in position. Will you let me try?"

Gram nodded her consent and he promptly grabbed her arm, cracking the wrist over his knee. Gruesome! As he dipped the plaster roll into water and began to wrap her wrist he asked, "Does it hurt too much? We can give you something for the pain."

Gram answered, "It smarts. That bandage makes it feel nice and warm." She took nothing for the pain. The next time she wandered off, she fell and broke her hip. Her youngest daughter, Evelyn was living with her then, but had to leave her alone while she went to work. Before Evelyn came back to live at six Ellen Street, Gram lived alone. Grandpa Elias died years before, while still working as janitor at Roosevelt School.

The family had to make a reluctant decision. For her safety, Gram was placed into care at the Belmont Home, a city run chronic care institution. Her diabetic condition caused her left lower leg to become gangrenous. Again, due to her advanced age, the medical doctors elected not to amputate and allowed the process to "demarcate." Her lower leg looked like she was wearing a dark brown leather boot: from her toes to her knee. She was frequently visited by three generations of her extended family.

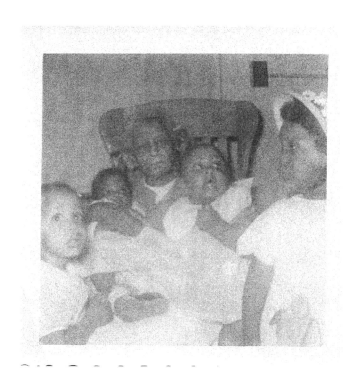

Laura F. Rickards with great granddaughters
L-R
Dorothy E. Brown Cox, Mia (Mary) E. Carter,
Elizabeth A. Brown Cronan, Laura F. (Carter) Rickards
At the Belmont Home circa 1961.

How different is life for the
great grandchildren of slaves?

Skokien knew community, yet never knew her parents. Her daughter, Mary Jane Lee, was a member of a community. The southern plantation community made attempts to separate black from white. The separation was manipulated and defiled at will. Black children were separated from black parents. White wives coped with their husbands "mixed" children.

Mary Jane Lee Washington's youngest daughter, Laura, had an early life much like her mother's. She was a chambermaid at the Groton Academy in Massachusetts, put "out to service" when seven years old! Her oldest brother, George, was left to serve on the plantation at about the same age.

Laura's daughter Dorothy, my mother, was able to complete eight years of elementary school and joined the labor force. She worked in a commercial laundry, cleaned office buildings and ran elevators. Her sister Evelyn, a Horace Mann honor student, finished high school, yet had a similar work life. She cleaned houses and offices, ran elevators, and spent years being a nanny. These intelligent, gifted women rose from legally sanctioned slavery or involuntary servitude, to social servitude. Dorothy's youngest daughter, this author, also cleaned houses to earn money and did childcare and was a licensed elevator operator!

Each generation of parents whatever their social class, whether black or white, immigrant or early settlers, aimed for the same goal. They were determined to make life better for their children. The move to Ellen Street was Elias's way of improving their lives. They rented number 4 Ellen Street and with the help of a white ally, Elias was able to buy a large tract of land on the northerly side of Ellen Street on the plan, known in November of 1912, as Benham Hill Park. That land still remains in the family and it was Laura's keen wit and stubborn courage that allowed that temporary home Elias built to remain standing until a new generation rebuilt upon the site in 1989.

Those social boundaries that limited the lives of colored people were still functioning in the late nineteen fifties and early sixties.

Four Generations of Mary Jane Lee Washington.

**Her daughter Laura Frances Washington Rickards (right),
and Laura's daughter Dorothy Lee Rickards Perkins
Barrow (center), and Dorothy's daughter Shirley Frances
Barrow Carter (left), and her daughter, Laura Frances
(Carter) Rickards on Dorothy's lap.
Portland, Maine, May 1958.**

The Inheritance

This great granddaughter of a slave can thank Skokien for surviving a life in which she was considered property, valued like a prize horse. Her ability to create a pseudo family and function in a parallel community of black folks gave me the gifts of endurance and resistance. Her daughter, Mary Jane Lee, bridged the gap between black and white, free and slave. She overcame the tethers of bondage going north to freedom. Her life of adjusting from Southern warmth and black community, gave me courage to find my way as a "minority" woman confronting the social barriers constructed by white Northern society.

I can thank Mary Jane Lee's youngest daughter Laura, for ambition and the righteous anger needed to resist oppression. She refused to allow the social isolation relegated to black society and never lived "separate" from white society. Her anger and rage at racism prompted her to carry a bull-whip to yank taunting, name calling boys from trees that lined the walk way to schools her daughters attended in Malden, Massachusetts. She fought the Worcester Public School Department and removed her girls from Thomas Street School where black and immigrant children were assigned. She kept them at home until the school department relented and allowed them to attend their neighborhood school on Abbott Street.

Malden, MA School class picture:
Elsie Viola Rickards third row/right.

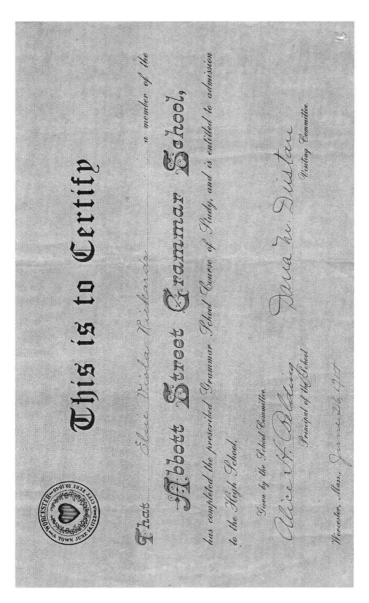

**Abbott Street School Completion Record,
Elsie Viola Rickards**

Class Photo
Dorothy Lee
Front Row

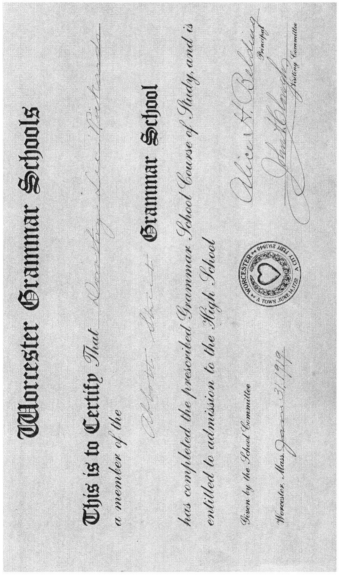

**Abbott Street School School Completion Record,
Dorothy Lee Rickards.**

Class Photo
Evelyn Louise
Second Row Middle

Dorothy's school life was fraught with many experiences of invalidation. She never went to high school. There were times when, Dorothy, Laura's middle daughter, appeared to acquiesce or accommodate. My mother's angst and anger seemed to smolder inside and explode when racism stared her in the face. If a clerk attempted to assist her only after all others were waited on, she would make a loud protest! Her life choices seemed like "acceptance" of the inevitable, acceptance of social miscasting of talented black people.

From her I learned to walk through irrational, racist life situations with the "appearance of conformity." I stuffed my rage and used Skokien's resistance and Mary Jane's determination to overcome the oppression, bridge both worlds, and take freedom as my inalienable right. The anger I held was against racism. No one could call me nigger and get away with it. I didn't have a whip, or the skill to use it against those who taunt. I was never alone in my battle against racism. I had collective wisdom, allies and the law. Accommodation never fit well on me. My skills are rooted in the resilience of my ancestors, their triumphs, the appearance of conformity, and the ability to negate the lies perpetuated by a racist society. With that inheritance, I never accept the role of victim.

These attributes from the past account for my liberated existence: property owner, possessor of multiple educational degrees, and mother of daughters who were bequeathed the same attributes, and have created lives that allow them to be contributors to a society still haunted by racism. These gifts from the past come with support from black and white communities, southern and northern—people of courage and conviction. Since

Mary Jane's birth in 1833 and my birth in 1931 much has changed. Racism is the same rotten, poison found in Césaire's poem, *Perdu*: screaming mothers, crying children in Darfur and many warring countries on the African continent and in the Americas. The atrocities of racism cannot be forgotten. But change has come.

On January 20, 2009, we the people of the United States of America inaugurated the forty-forth president: a black man, named Barack Hussein Obama. The disrespect directed at him is racist. This statement is not factual yet it is true.

A Note from the Author

Alex Haley's *Roots* fired this book, but the true genesis began many years before when I sat at my Grandmother's feet, listening to her story of her family, her beginnings. I could predict where the story would begin and end, yet with each retelling it held more power, more pride, and more conviction than the time before. It became my story and I claimed the same pride that Gram portrayed.

By 1977, I had collected a series of notes, refined them twice and noticed they had become rather comprehensive. I can thank my daughters, Laura and Mia, and their cousin Dorothy for my collection. Each had taken college courses requiring "cultural background, family information and history." It was the year my mother died. Genealogy became important, almost urgent. My niece returned all my notes and a tape I had made in celebration of my mother's life. The book, *Fleming's Red-Headed Nigger* was born.

Researching, gathering documents, and sharing oral history with other relatives excited me and whet my appetite for discovery. Research confirmed and verified much of my grandmother's stories. Mary Jane Lee Washington, my great grandmother, became a vital character in my book.

I used the word nigger in the title of the first draft: a direct quote from my grandmother's telling of her mother's youth on the plantation.

"He'd ride up to the quarters and call out, 'Send out my red headed nigger!' " She used the word as if it wasn't a bad thing, for a white man, a man reported to be Robert E. Lee, to call for his issue to come out and visit with him! Because she used the word with such abandon, I used it for the title. It was such an unimaginable situation, such a shocking story that it made the word acceptable in my mind. The reader would be as amazed at its use as I was. My grandmother used it. Somehow, that made it "authentic," even though it shocked me when she used it! It is not a nice word, the word, nigger.

At my youngest daughter Mia's home in Austin Texas, I read a poem by Aimé Césaire. The word Nigger in my book felt risqué, until I read *"Word"* in Césaire's *Perdu.*[3] It felt like Mary Jane Lee's slave mother was screaming at me from an unknown grave. To date, I do not know the name of her slave mother, known to the reader as Skokien, but Césaire's poem exploded *the word* into its full meaning and ugliness.

---

[3]Clayton Eshleman and Annette Smith, "Word," in The Collected Poetry, AiméCésaire (Los Angeles, University of California Press, 1983), 229-233.

The word nigger	le mot nègre
Emerged fully armed	sorti tout armé
from the howling	du hurlement

Of a poisonous flower	d'une fleur vénéneuse
The word nigger	le mot nègre
All filthy with	tout pouacre de
parasites	parasites

The word nigger	le mot nègre
Loaded with roaming bandits	tout plein de brigands
	qui rôdent

With screaming mothers	des mères qui crient
Crying children	d'enfents qui crient
The word nigger	le mot nègre
A sizzling of flesh and	un grésillement de
horny matter	chairs qui brùlent

Burning, acrid	âcre et de corne
The word nigger	le mot nègre
Like the sun bleeding	com le soleil qui saigne
from its claw	de la griffe

| Onto the sidewalk of clouds | sur le trottoir des |
| | nuages |

The word nigger	le mot nègre
Like the last laugh calved by	comme ler dernier rire
innocence	vélé de l'innocence

I believed my book had a powerful title. A conversation with my grand nephew, Raphael, convinced me that the term nigger is still offensive—not a proper title for a family history. After much discussion, I shared my thinking about using *The Roan,* an equine reference to the combined tones of red, white and brown. It symbolizes Mary Jane Lee: a slave child with red hair, brown mother, and a white father, a horse as metaphor for a slave woman who labored like a valued domestic animal, and was considered chattel. We agreed to change the title to *The Roan.*

Biblographical Note

The reader will note many references in this book are taken from family correspondence along with hospital records, doctoral dissertations and historical websites. Photocopies of significant records and other documents will appear before the listing of books, articles and web sites.

Death Certificates: Mary Jane Lee Washington, George T. Washington, Laura Frances Washington Rickards, Elias Edward Rickards

Hand Written & Typed Account of *Cape News:* Oldest Resident of Cape is 95

Tewksbury Hospital Medical Record: Mary Jane Lee Washington

Elias Rickards' Western Union Telegraph to Laura in Malden

The Commonwealth of Massachusetts

UNITED STATES OF AMERICA.

COPY OF RECORD OF DEATH

.........................TOWN..........of..........TEWKSBURY...........................

I, the undersigned, hereby certify that I am clerk of the ......Town........of....Tewksbury..............
that as such I have custody of the records of deaths required by law to be kept in my office;
that among such records is one relating to the death of
....MARY J. WASHINGTON...
and that the following is a true copy of so much of said record as relates to said death, namely;

Date of death.............December 30, 1896..

Place of death.............Tewksbury, Ma...

Name ....Mary J. Washington..
     If divorced is a married, widowed or divorced woman, give also maiden name and name of husband.

Sex ....Female.........Color.....Black...

Single, Married, Widowed or Divorced ....Married........................

Husband or Wife of ....--..

Age ....67........ Years .....--......... Months .....--....... Days

Residence...--..

Occupation...--..

U.S. War Veteran ....--...
                                              Specify War

Place of Birth.......--...

FATHER	MOTHER
Name ....--.........	Full Maiden Name.........--.........
Place of Birth.......--.........	Place of Birth.........--.........

Cause of Death ...Debility..

Type of Disposition.......--............ Place and Location.....Groton,, MA.....................

Date of Record....--..

(SEAL)

And I do hereby certify that the foregoing is a true copy from said records.

Witness my hand and seal of said ....Town.....of....Tewksbury...........

on this .....18th.......day of.....May........19 95

Elizabeth A. Carey

Clerk

Year....................

Vol......................

Page....................

No.......................

FORM S 431 A. M. SULKIN   REVISED 1983

180

The Commonwealth of Massachusetts

UNITED STATES OF AMERICA.

COPY OF RECORD OF DEATH

Town .... of .... Barnstable ....

I, the undersigned, hereby certify that I am clerk of the ...Town............of....Barnstable............
that as such I have custody of the records of deaths required by law to be kept in my office;
that among such records is one relating to the death of
..................George Washington..
and that the following is a true copy of so much of said record as relates to said death, namely;

Date of death............October 13, 1911..
Place of death............Barnstable..

Name .....George Washington..
<small>If deceased is a married, widowed or divorced woman, give also maiden name and name of husband.</small>
Sex ..... Male................Color .. Colored................................
Single, Married, Widowed or Divorced ......Widowed............................
Husband or Wife of ....unknown..
Age ....88.... Years .... Months .... Days
Residence ....Barnstable..
Occupation........Laborer..
U.S. War Veteran ....."...
<small>Specify War</small>
Place of Birth....Maryland..

FATHER	MOTHER
Name ....James Washington................	Full Maiden Name. ......Unknown................
Place of Birth...... Unknown................	Place of Birth............Unknown................

Cause of Death ......Senile Apoplexy..
Type of Disposition........":................... Place and Location,..... South Street, Hyannis.............
Date of Record......November 4, 1911..

And I do hereby certify that the foregoing is a true copy from said records.

Witness my hand and seal of said ....Town....of....Barnstable................

on this........5th................day of ..August................19 98

(SEAL)

Year......1911........
Vol..........24..........
Page........85..........
No........72..........

Linda S. Hutchenride Clerk

FORM 431 HOBBS & WARREN, INC. PUBLISHERS REVISED 1983

181

Commonwealth of Massachusetts

City of Worcester
CITY CLERK DEPARTMENT

May 4, 1995

I, DAVID J. RUSHFORD, hereby certify that I hold the office of Assistant City Clerk, and have the custody of the Records of this City relating to Deaths, and that the following is a copy from the records of Deaths in said city.

Date of Death......July 3, 1962....... { If U.S. War Veteran Specify War

Name of Deceased.......Laura E. (Washington) Rickards

Sex...Female...Condition...Widowed....Age 86...years 9...months 12...days

Disease or Cause of Death } Arteriosclerotic heart disease. Gen. arteriosclerosis. Diabetes mellitus.

Residence........Worcester, Massachusetts

Occupation......Housewife........Name of Husband, or Wife....Elias E. Rickards

Place of Death.....Worcester, MA...Place of Birth....Boston, MA

Name of Father.....George Washington

Birthplace of Father......Unknown

Name of Mother......Mary J. Lee

Birthplace of Mother.......Unknown

Place of Burial or Cremation.....Hope Cemetery, Worcester, Massachusetts

Date of Record........July 5, 1962

kp

IN WITNESS WHEREOF I hereunto set my hand and seal of said City, the day and year first above written.

_____
Assistant City Clerk.

182

Commonwealth of Massachusetts

City of Worcester
CITY CLERK DEPARTMENT

May 4, 1995

I, DAVID J. RUSHFORD, hereby certify that I hold the office of Assistant City Clerk, and have the custody of the Records of this City relating to Deaths, and that the following is a copy from the records of Deaths in said city.

Date of Death.......... November 1, 1937   { If U. S. War Veteran — — —   Specify War

Name of Deceased...... Elias E. Rickards

Sex...... Male   Condition...... Married   Age...... 70 ...years...1...months...4...days

Disease or Cause of Death } Arteriosclerosis. Coronary Sclerosis. Arteriosclerotic Myocardial Degeneration. Diabetes Mellitus. Prostatic Hypertrophy.

Residence...... Worcester, Massachusetts

Occupation...... Janitor ......Name of Husband, or Wife...... — — —

Place of Death...... Worcester, MA   Place of Birth...... Boston, MA

Name of Father...... Elias Rickards

Birthplace of Father...... Pennsylvania

Name of Mother...... Unknown

Birthplace of Mother...... Pennsylvania

Place of Burial or Cremation...... Hope Cemetery, Worcester, Massachusetts

Date of Record...... November 3, 1937

kp

IN WITNESS WHEREOF I hereunto set my hand and seal of said City, the day and year first above written.

Assistant City Clerk.

Oldest Resident of Cape is 96 —

Hyannisport Oct-13. Out on the Hyannisport and Hyannis was
In a little settlement call Happy Hollow, the original sight.
Of the first Village on cape cod, lives the oldest resident
George Washington. who has just celebrated his 95 —
Birthday. not a day goes by but he takes a walk
of two to three miles. he was Born in Howard county
Maryland. Oct-20-1813 on the plantation of Beny Crapster
Where he work'd until the age of 17. when he sold on the
Block for 600 dollars to a son of his first owner.
& six hundred
After the sale I was put in gans of slaves and sent
To Fredricksberg county to work on a farm
The work was hard and my new master was a driver
So I thought I would runaway which I did. I went to
Baltimore and there ship'd on a Vessel bound fa
England we went to sea about two years when we landed
At a port in S. Carolinee and I was taken to the old
Plantation again and this time with a ball and chain
I was there about three years. and I married a slave
Girl on the next plantation one day I asked my master
If I could raise the money what he would take for me
And he say'd seven hundred I told him I knew a man
That would put up that money and wanted a day
off to go and see him which he did the first thing I did
After I got off of the plantation was to get that ball off
of my leg then I made for the swamp with my

184

mind made up never to go back alive I lived in the
Swamp for over three weeks before I had a chance to
Work north. and when I got on the road I never stoped
Till I got to St. Johns N.B. after I got there I wrote
my Wife so after I got to Boston and she got her
Fredon she came to Boston. one day I was down
On Alantic Ave when a man came along and
Asked me if I would work fo him. he took me down
To Cape Cod. we had 12 Children in all I have 28
Grandchildren and 20 Great grand children
My Wife died 8 years ago at the age of 63 I
Hope to live to be a 100. then I would be wiling to
Give up my work to younger hands
The house in Washingto I live in is the first expres
Office that was in the state of Mass known as
Houtots expres station Mr Gould the originator
Of the buisness was the same man that mail
from G Chicago to Boston I have ben South since
The war and we live down there a few years then back
To Boston. then I bought a fam up in Roylston but
It was to far from my work so I move to Readsvill mass
then to Charkton. after awhile I bought a place in
Shirley and worked in a mill in N. Groton for 5 years
and went back to Boston. and I went back to England
twice. now I am here to stay

185

Hyannisport - Oct. 13. Out on the Hyannisport and Hyannis road,
in a little settlement called Happy Hollow, the original site of
the first village on Cape Cod, lives the oldest resident, George
Washington, who has just celebrated his 95th birthday. Not a day
goes by but he takes a walk of two or three miles. He was born in
Howard County, Maryland, October 20, 1813, on the plantation of
Benj. Crapster, where he worked until the age of 17, when he was
sold on the block for six hundred (600) dollars to a son of his
first owner.

"After the sale I was put in _____ of slaves and sent to Fredericksburg
County to work on a farm. The work was hard and my new master was
a driver. So I thought I would run away, which I did. I went to
Baltimore and there shipped on a vessel bound for England. We
were at sea about two years. When we landed at a port in South
Carolina, I was taken to the old plantation and this time with a
ball and chain. I lived there about three years and I married a
slave girl on the next plantation. One day I asked my master if I
could raise the money, what he would take for me, and he said
seven hundred (700) dollars. I told him I knew a man that would
put up that money and wanted a day off to go and see him, which
he he did. The first thing I did after I got off the plantation
was to get that ball off my leg. Then I made for the swamp with
my mind made up never to go back alive. I lived in the swamp for
over three weeks before I had a chance to work north, and when I
got on the road I never stopped till I got to St. John, N.B.
After I got there I wrote my wife so after I got to Boston and she

186

got her freedom, she came to Boston. One day I was down on
Atlantic Avenue when a man came along and asked me if I would
work for him. He took me down to Cape Cod. We had twelve (12)
children. In all I have 28 grandchildren and 29 great grandchildren. My wife died eight (8) years ago at the age of 63.
I hope to live to be 100. Then I would be willing to give up
my work to younger hands.

The house the Washingtons live in is the first express office
that was in the State of Massachusetts, known as Gould's Express
Station. Mr. Gould, the originator of the business was the same
man that brought the mail from Chicago to Boston.

I have been south once since the war, and we lived down there
a few years, then back to Boston. Then I bought a farm up in
Royalston, bit it was too far from my work, so I moved to Readville,
Mass. Then to Charlestown. After a while I bought a place in
Shirley and worked in a mill in W. Groton for five years, and then
went back to Boston, Mass. I went back to England twice. Now I
am hereto stay.

I never went to school, but I learned to read and write."

Civil Hist.

Reg. No. *106689* Name, *Mary J. Washington*

Birthplace. — Occupation, —

Admitted *Dec 2nd* 1896

Religion. —

Age. *55* Color. *White*

Social Condition. —

Parents' Names. — Parents' Birthplace. —

Address of Friends. —

Previous Record. See Vol. v Page v Previous Diagnosis. v

Family Hist. *Negative*

Previous Sickness.

Venereal Hist.

Subj. Symp. *Was hurt last night by another patient and has a black eye at present*

Phys. Exam. Temp. Pulse, Weight, Urine,

PHYS EXAM *Fair developed and emaciated feeble*

CHEST&ABDOMEN *Lungs Heart and abdomen negative*

FACE *Extensive contusion of face right eyelid, badly swollen Bridge of nose broken*

HEAD *Depression over margin of right parietal and frontal bone Dr Inch was called in consultation and cut down and bupled pericher but there was no fracture or depn of skull it was simply a depression of bone wound sewed up.*

EYES *Pupils react to light   are equal arms and fingers twitch*

188

Patient can only be aroused enough to take nourish-
ment and medicine.
Patient is very stupid
doing well
Took out stitches and found wound healed.
Patient sat up a little while yesterday
Patient sits up a little but is very weak.
Patient has been sitting up every day but now seems
so weak that it is hard to make her do it

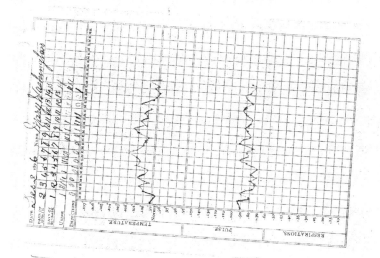

Debility Confusion of Head

Date. Dec 30 1896   Condition. Died   Weight.

Physical Exam: Fairly developed and emaciated feeble.

Chest and Abdomen: Lungs Heart and abdomen negative.

Face: Extensive contusion of face right eyelid badly
         swollen. Bridge of nose broken.

Head: Depression over margin of right parietal and frontal
         bone. Dr. Irish was called in consultation and cut
         down and lifted perioustum but there was no fracture
         or depression of skull. It was simply a depression
         of tissue wound sewed up.

Eyes: Pupils react to light; are equal.

         Arms and fingers twitch.

Patient can only be aroused enough to take nourishment
and medicine.

Patient is very stupid.
Doing well.
Took out stitches and found wound healed.
Patient sat up a little while yesterday.
Patient sits up a little but is very weak.

Patient has been sitting up every day but now seems so weak
that it is hard to make her do it.

Ms. Carter: I have typed this for you as copy of Mary Jane
Lee Washington's written pages are hard to read.

copy sent to Atty. Michael Price on 9-20-89/mc with typed copy
of the two pages of medical on Mary J. L. Washington/mc

Admitting Card

Reg. No.	4/6/60
Insane No.	2213
Name	Washington, Mary J. L.
Date, Age	June 15, 1896 67
Birthplace	Washington, D.C.
Condition	Insane
Occupation	None
	Male
Last former No.	
Personal peculiarities	Colored
Discha	Dec 30/96
Died	Su. Ob. v. Pg.

191

THE WESTERN UNION TELEGRAPH COMPANY
INCORPORATED

25,000 OFFICES IN AMERICA.   CABLE SERVICE TO ALL THE WORLD

This Company TRANSMITS and DELIVERS messages only on conditions limiting its liability, which have been assented to by the sender of the following message.
Errors can be guarded against only by repeating a message back to the sending station for comparison, and the Company will not hold itself liable for errors or delays in transmission or delivery of Unrepeated Messages, beyond the amount of tolls paid thereon, nor in any case beyond the sum of Fifty Dollars, at which, unless otherwise stated below, this message has been valued by the sender thereof, nor in any case where the claim is not presented in writing within sixty days after the message is filed with the Company for transmission.
This is an UNREPEATED MESSAGE, and is delivered by request of the sender, under the conditions named above.

THEO. N. VAIL, PRESIDENT   BELVIDERE BROOKS, GENERAL MANAGER

RECEIVED AT

5B R 8   913AM

Worcester, Mass. Dec. 2,

Mrs. L. F. Rickards, 442 Eastern Ave., Malden, Mass.

Look up house leave everything come today sure.

E. E. Rickards...927AM

192

TELEGRAPH AND CABLE SERVICE TO ALL THE WORLD.

THE WESTERN UNION TELEGRAPH CO.

INCORPORATED

NUMBER

513

CHARGES

Mr L F Rickea

4¾V Eastern Ar

CHARGES TO MESSENGER UNLESS WRITTEN IN INK IN DELIVERY BOOK.

193

Books

Andrews, Frederick and Paul, T. Owen. *Black Language.*
    Los Angeles: Seymour-Smith, 1973.
Bancroft, Frederick. *Slave Trading in the Old South.*
    New York: Unger Publishing Co., 1931, 1959.
Boyer, H. C. "Climbing' Up D' Mountain," *Lift Every Voice and
    Sing 11*. New York: The Church Pension Fund, 1993.
Calhoun, Jeanne A. *The African American Experience at
    Stratford:* 1782. Princeton Public Library.
Cather, Willa. *Sapphira and the Slave Girl.*
    New York. New York: Alfred A. Knopf Inc., 1976.
Chestnutt, Charles W. *The Conjure Woman and Other Conjure
    Tales.* London: Duke University Press, 1993.
Douglas, Frederick. *Life and Times of Frederick Douglas.*
    London: Collier-McMillan, 1892.
Eshleman, C. and A. Smith. *The Collected Poetry
    Aime´Ce´saire.* California: University of California
    Press, Berkeley and Los Angeles, 1983.
Franklin, John Hope and Alfred A. Moss Jr. *From Slavery to
    Freedom: A History of African Americans.*
    New York: McGraw-Hill, 1994.
Gordon-Reed, Annette. *The Hemmings of Monticello: An
    American Family.*
    New York: W.W. Norton & Company, 2008.

Herman, Lewis and Marguerite Shalett Herman. *American Dialects: A Manual for Actors, Directors, and Writers.* New York: Routledge, 1997.

Jacobs, Harriet. Incidents *Life of a Slave Girl Written by Herself.* Cambridge: Harvard University Press, 1987.

Lee, Robert E. Jr. *Recollections and Letters of General Robert E. Lee.* Charleston: Nabu Press, 2010.

Major, Clarence. *Juba to Jive: A Dictionary of American Slang.* New York: Penguin, 1994.

Oikle, Alvin F. *The Man with the Branded Hand.* Everett, MA: Slater Publishing, 1998.

Taylor, Quintard. *In Search of the Racial Frontier.* New York: W.W. Norton & Company, 1999.

The Book of Knowledge: The Children' Encyclopedia Vol. 4. New York: Grolier, 1945.

Wilkerson, Isabel. *The Warmth of Other Suns.* New York: Random House, 2010.

Articles

Cooling Springs Farm. "The History of Cooling Spring Farm
and the Michael Family in the Underground
Railroad." http://www.coolingsprings.org.

Corrigan, M.E. *Slavery and Freedom on the Middle Ground:
Maryland during the Nineteenth Century,* Diss.
Yale University, 1985. New Haven, CT.

Corrigan, Mary Beth, PhD. *A Social Union of Heart and Effort:
The African American Family in the District of
Columbia on the Eve of Emancipation.* Diss.
University of Maryland, 1996. College Park, MD.

Emmitsburg Area Historical Society, "Life in Emmitsburg in
the 1800's Farm Life & Political Campaigns."
http://www.emmitsburg.net/archive_list/articles/his
tory/chronical_life_in_1800/farm_life.htm.

Gillette, Howard Jr. "Southern City, National Ambition:
The Growth of Early Washington, DC 1800-1860."
Washington History Vol. 8, No. 1 (1995): 70-73.

Larjent, Kimberly J. "The Life of Mary Custas Lee."
http://ehistory.osu.edu/osu/default.cfm.

Leach, Jim. "Civility in a Fractured Society." *AARP Bulletin*
(October 2010): 38.

Links to the Past. "Beginnings of the Underground Railroad
across Southeastern Ohio."

http://www.henryrobertburke.com/id14.html.

Millersville University. "The Life of William Parker and His
Impact on the Christiana Riot,"
http://muweb.millersville.edu/~ugrr/christiana/
Parker.html.

Morales, Leslie Anderson. "The Virginia Slave Birth Index,
1853-1865: How 19th Century Data Became a 21st
Century Research Tool." Presentation at Alexandria
Library Afro-American Historical and Genealogy
Annual Conference, October 2007.

Shewmake, Edwin Francis. *English Pronunciation in Virginia.*
Diss. Davidson College 1927.
Davidson, North Carolina.

Special Collections, Leyburn Library, Washington and Lee
University. "Lee Papers."
http://miley.wlu.edu/LeePapers/.

Warnick, Florence. "Dialect of Garrett County Maryland."
Privately Printed, 1942.

Wikipedia. "African American Vernacular English."
http://en.wikipedia.org/wiki/African_American_
Vernacular_English.

Wikipedia. "Culture of the Southern United States."
http://en.wikipedia.org/wiki/Culture_of_the_
Southern_United_States .

Williams, Dera, post to AfriGeneas Books-Authors-Reviews
Forum, "[History] The Pearl: A Failed Slave Escape on
the Potomac," June 11, 2006, http://www.afrige
neas.com/forum-books/index.cgi?md=read;id=1523

Individual Letters

Index of Photographs

Page:

Evelyn Louise Rickards, second row center

Front Book Cover Photo: Portrait of Mary Jane Lee Washington

Back of Book: DNA matrilineal line from the oldest African ancestor to Mary Jane Lee Washington to one of her daughters, Laura Frances Washington Rickards to one of her daughters, Dorothy Lee Rickards Perkins Barrow to one of her daughters, Shirley Frances Barrow Carter to one of her daughters, Mia Elizabeth Carter to her daughter, Ariane Alexis Reis Corcoran.

NB* The author's matrilineal DNA which traces the mother, of the mother, of the mother, etc. was professionally done by Dr. Rick Kittles, Scientific Director of African Ancestry, Inc. and also Co-Director of Molecular Genetics at the National Genome Center at Howard University.

Mary Jane Lee had more than one daughter: Sarah, Zilpha, Helen, Caroline, and Laura. Their DNA also goes to the same Ticar strain as does the daughters of Laura Washington Rickards: Elsie, Dorothy, and Evelyn. The same for the daughters of Elsie: Lorraine and Joyce, and the daughters of Dorothy: Lois, Audrey, and Shirley, and the daughters of Lois: Cortelle, Claudia, Lois and Debra, and the daughters of Audrey: Dorothy, Elizabeth, Diane and Susanne, and the daughters of Shirley: Laura and Mia, and the daughter of Mia, Ariane!

Boston June 29. 90.

My Dear Laura

Yours at hand
Dear Babe and I am
very glad to hear from
you and that you are
better and I hope you
continue to gain and also
I wish if you think of any
thing that you may want
from the city you must
let me know it and I will
be more than pleased to get

Elias Rickards Letter—page 1.

for you. Dearest Babe I
have work very hard since I
last saw you, our business
is at it hight now. I have had
to work very late night, but
I guess that it will not hold
on longer than usual. Charles
Frank and I was out
Sunday to Everett and Malden
looking over a few houses
for our future homes but
didn't see one that quite
suited, and next Sunday
we are to go to Revere
Highlands. Dear Babe I
would like very much

Elias Rickards Letter—page 2.

to spend the Fourth
with you but I cannot I
have to work as it is
our busiest day of season
I will be up to see
you any way the third
Sunday of month if not
sooner. My sister Grace
I guess will start next
week on a pleasure trip to
Philadelphia. Pa. She and
her companion Miss Flora Simms
are go together for a 8 week.
Dear Babe I sent the parcell
to last Monday and I hope

Elias Rickards Letter—page 3.

you have received it
allright. you will find
enclosed a small package
address to Burt will you
please say for me that is the
Rivets for his horse harness I
promised him. I will enclose
a circular of the Odd Fellow
Picnic and I hope you will
go to that as I want you to
anyway. I send you a program
of unvieling of Farragut Statue
Thursday in So. Boston and
the lodge is going on Fourth
to Newburyport Mass to the
unvieling of Wm L. Garrison
Statue

Elias Rickards Letter—page 4.

All at present with love to you and family from all also love and many kiss from yours

Yours Only

Elias H. Rickards.

Miss L. T. Washington

Pepperell Centre,

Mass.

Elias Rickards Letter—page 5 & envelope.

Pepperell June 1/93

Dear Elias

Received your
loving letter with much
pleasure, it found us
all well, as I hope
this one will find you.
I suppose you have
received my last
letter but this time
I know I ought to
have written before,
but I was so busy,
there is so much to
do in such a large

family, there are eleven
of us you know. We,
that is, Helen, & and
the children all but
the baby went to
meeting this morning.
The minister preached
a beautiful sermon
to the children. They
are all out doors under
the trees but Albert
and I. Albert is
asleep. We were
all surprised to hear
of the death of your
father, although we
knew he had been
sick so long. They
have had one case

of the Small pox
her Pepperell, but I
guess it won't amount
to anything more
she / It was a woman
; is dead. The doctor
came down Ned-
nesday and
vaccinated the
children he said
he didn't think
they would have
any more cases, a
great many don't
believe it was the
small pox. Now I
will close with love
from all to all Yours
lovingly L. H. Washington

Laura Washington Letter—page 3.

Laura Washington envelope.

Whitman Mass.
May. 1st. 1907.

Mr. O.E. Pickards.
Brockton.

Dear Sir...
At Our Meeting of the Trustees
Monday Evening It. was thought
that we would make a change
in our Janitor Work. at present.
We. feel very sorry that we
have to make the change for.
every thing has been O.K. up
to the time of the break.
Now. I will meet you at
the Church. to night Wednesday
evening at. 6 o'clock. and fix.

Trustee Letter—page 2.

2.

you for your past work to-
date. and bring your Keys
with you. Hoping that this
will not put you out at all.
I remain.

Very truly Yours
Geo. A Stevens Treas.

After 5 days, return to

804

WHITMAN, MASS.

WHITMAN
MAY
1
7AM
1907
MASS.

2

Mr. C.C. Rickards
#131 Elsworth St..
Brockton.
mass.

Trustee Letter—page 2 & envelope.

CPSIA information can be obtained at www.ICGtesting.com
Printed in the USA
BVOW012212281012

304157BV00007B/1/P